# BE THOU PRESENT:
## Prayers, Litanies, and Hymns
## for Christian Worship

# BE THOU PRESENT:
## Prayers, Litanies, and Hymns
## for Christian Worship

## Peggy A. Haymes

Smyth & Helwys Publishing, Inc.®
Macon, Georgia

ISBN 1-880837-90-0

The paper used in this publication meets the minimum
requirements of American Standard for Information
Sciences—Permanence of paper for Printed Library Materials,
ANSI Z39.48–1984.

*Library of Congress Cataloging-in-Publication Data*

Haymes, Peggy A.
    Be Thou present : prayers, litanies, and hymns for Christian
worship / by Peggy A. Haymes.
    x + 101 pp.              6 X 9"   (15 X 23 cm.)
    ISBN 1-880837-90-0
    1. Public worship—Baptists. 2. Prayers. 3. Prayer—Baptists.
I. Title.
BX6337.H35  1994
264'.061013—dc                                    93–48139

                                                    CIP

# Contents

# Preface

"I was thinking the other day," a friend remarked, "that when we pray in our worship services we don't really need to ask God to be present. God is already there, waiting to meet us."

He had a point. And yet, as I have prepared prayers for worship, I find myself coming back again and again to the same cry: "Be Thou present." Perhaps God does not need our invitation, but we need to voice our prayer. As in all of our prayers—even though God may already know our hearts—we still need to voice our needs and fears, hopes and hurts.

That is something of what this book of worship resources is all about. Through the words that are spoken and sung, the community of faith gives voice to the cries of its heart. We share in both praise and petition, confession and commitment. This collection contains resources for the "ordinary" days, prayers of invocation and confession and offertory prayers. It also includes resources for special times in the church's life, whether the seasons of Advent and Lent or times of commissioning and dedication.

I owe a word of gratitude to many persons for their help and support in the preparation of this book: The members of my home church (First Baptist Church of Winston-Salem, North Carolina) encouraged a high school student who was beginning to write prayers for worship. I had the privilege of helping to lead in worship services for six years while I was on the staff of College Park Baptist Church, Greensboro, North Carolina. I am indebted to James M. Pitts and the late L. D. Johnson, chaplains of Furman University; while working with them in planning the university worship services, the dream for this book was born. Thanks go to C. Michael Hawn who taught me about hymnody and served as constructive critic of my first hymn-writing efforts. Also, a special word of appreciation goes to Bob and Hessie Williams for their help in proofreading my manuscript. Finally, I would like to express my thanks to my family members for their support and to my friends at Smyth and Helwys for both their encouragement of and patience with this project.

*Peggy A. Haymes*
*Greensboro, North Carolina*

# Foreword

In the latter part of the book of Psalms are fifteen short "Songs of Ascent"—songs written as worshipers made the journey to the temple in Jerusalem. These Songs of Ascent begin in solitude and end in corporate worship. The first one, for example, is Psalm 120, which begins:

> In my distress I cry to the Lord,
>     that he may answer me:
> "Deliver me, O Lord,
>     from lying lips,
>     from a deceitful tongue."
>         (Ps 120:1)

Far more familiar are the opening verses of the next psalm (121):

> I lift up my eyes to the hills—
>     from where will my help come?
> My help comes from the Lord,
>     who made heaven and earth.

Here are the private prayers of a pilgrim on the way to worship in Jerusalem. But soon the mood of the psalms changes. By the time we come to the end of the "Songs of Ascent," the worship is corporate, not private:

> How very good and pleasant it is
>     when kindred live together in unity!
> It is like the precious oil on the head,
>     running down upon the beard,
> on the beard of Aaron,
>     running down over the collar of his robes.
>         (Ps 133:1–2)

And the last psalm in the collection is even more corporate in tone:

> Come, bless the Lord, all you
>     servants of the Lord,
> who stand by night in the house of the Lord!
> Life up your hands to the holy place,
>     and bless the Lord!
>                     (Ps 134:1-2)

From a single soul crying out in distress on the way to worship (Ps 120), we move to the final image of hundreds of hands lifted up to God in corporate prayer (Ps 134). The spiritual needs of the *individual* are at the beginning; the *corporate* confidence of the congregation is at the end.

We all live in this tension of individual and corporate, private and public, "I-ness" and "we-ness," autonomy and community. What has loosely been called "spirituality" in recent years has taken on renewed interest among people of both Christian and Jewish heritage, as well as among those who have separated themselves from any worshiping community. But "spirituality" has often been described as private in emphasis, as if spiritual growth is something accomplished only by the individual, alone with God.

Corporate worship, on the other hand, stands in weekly testimony that spirituality is also community, that "I" am also part of a "we," and that in the community of believers I am more complete and fulfilled than if I tried to go it alone.

I mention this whole issue of individual versus corporate spirituality because I believe that Peggy Haymes is lifting a much-needed banner for corporate worship in this book. These are "we" prayers, not "I" prayers. By the very pronoun "we" they testify to that too often neglected need for companionship on the journey, as well as to our need for God.

The free church tradition from which Peggy Haymes comes has tended to downplay the priestly role of the worship leader. There has never been a problem with the prophetic role, however. Baptists have thought nothing of spending ten to fifteen hours a week preparing a sermon, fully expecting the influence of the Spirit in preparation. Some have sworn by Fosdick's unthinkable rule of thumb for sermon preparation: namely one hour of preparation for every minute of delivery!

But leading in public prayer has been another matter altogether. Prepared prayers have not been considered spiritual in that tradition. To be spiritual, they had to be spontaneous. Considered even worse have been prayers that were read; they were downright heretical, no matter how beautiful or meaningful the wording. It never seemed to occur to those in that tradition that there was any contradiction in the belief that God can inspire sermons during preparation, but God certainly could not inspire prayers during preparation.

But somewhere along the way, thoughtful people growing up in that tradition began to see the contradiction. Peggy Haymes is among them. A wonderful sense of reverence is coupled with a sense of the everyday pressures and burdens of people in these prayers. The prayers are often poetic in form, and they possess a keen sense of what I would call the rhythm of worship. An appropriateness, a rightness about these prayers, make them useful in any church that places corporate prayer as important.

I have a friend who is the chair of a hymnbook revision committee for his denomination. One of the letters his committee received regarding the new hymnbook in process was this one-liner: "Please make them singable!" It was a heartfelt call from someone who places great value on congregational singing.

You could say that these prayers are "prayable." I know because I spent a couple of months using many of them in the church I serve, and I have found them to be so. They speak to our hearts and minds; they call forth the congregational "Amen"; and they express in clear and simple language just the right words of praise and confession, thanksgiving and intercession for which the church longs in corporate worship.

*Thomas R. McKibbens, Senior Minister*
*First Baptist Church in Newton*
*Newton Centre, Massachusetts*

# Calls to Worship

Leader: We come this morning to worship the God made known in Christ Jesus.

**People: We come seeking the Christ, the Light of the world.**

Leader: We come to worship God, and to seek God's presence.

**People: Our eyes are used to the darkness. The light of God's presence may be painfully bright.**

Leader: Our lives have grown easy in the darkness. The light of God's presence may be uncomfortable.

**People: Even so, we come to worship.**
**Even so, we seek God's presence, for in this Light are our lives.**

Leader: Let us worship God together.

✝✝✝

Leader: Grace to you, and peace from God and our Lord Jesus Christ.

**People: The peace of our Lord be with you.**

Leader: We gather to worship with joy and not fear, for by the power of God's love we have been reconciled to God.

**People: "By grace we have been saved by faith, and this is not our own doing, it is a gift from God." (Eph 2:8)**

Leader: "For you know the grace of our Lord Jesus Christ, that though he was rich, yet for your sake he became poor, so that by his poverty you might become rich." (2 Cor 8:9)

**All: Let us worship our God who has brought us peace and given us life.**

✝✝✝

| Leader: | God who is the source of all life |
|---|---|
| **People:** | **And the lover of all creation,** |
| Leader: | You are a God of mystery. |
| **People:** | **May our worship be filled with wonder.** |
| Leader: | You are a God of truth. |
| **People:** | **In our worship we seek the truth about who we are and whose we are.** |
| Leader: | You are a God of wisdom. |
| **People:** | **May we not settle for merely being clever.** |
| Leader: | You are a God whose kingdom has no end. |
| **People:** | **May we be kingdom people.** |
| **All:** | **Amen.** |

†††

| Leader: | Come, let us worship the Lord our God. |
|---|---|
| **People:** | **For great is the Lord, and greatly to be praised.** |
| Leader: | In our worship, may our eyes be opened this day |
| **People:** | **That we might see the beauty and bounty of God's gifts.** |
| Leader: | May our eyes be opened this day |
| **People:** | **That we might see our need for God's grace.** |
| Leader: | May our eyes be opened this day |
| **People:** | **That we might see those who are in need.** |
| Leader: | May our eyes be opened this day |
| **People:** | **That we might worship God in spirit and in truth, and having worshiped, that we might serve God with faith and compassion.** |
| Leader: | Come, let us worship the Lord our God. |

†††

Leader: By the power of God, the heavens and the earth and all of creation came to be.

People: **By the power of God, a slave people were delivered from the hand of Pharaoh to become God's people.**

Leader: By the power of God, the Word became flesh and dwelt among us.

People: **By the power of God, the finality of death was conquered by life.**

Leader: Come, let us worship our God who gives strength to the weary and power to the faint.

ттт

Leader: Grace to you, and peace from him who was, and is, and who is to come, the Alpha and the Omega, the beginning and the end.

People: **Let us rejoice, for the Christ who saved us and freed us from our sins shall yet come again.**

Leader: And for those who serve the Lord, night will be no more; they need no light of lamp or sun, for the Lord God will be their light.

People: **Even so, Lord Jesus, quickly come.**
(Adapted from Rev 1 and 22)

ттт

Leader: We are gathered for worship.

People: **There is much to do in this world, for the hungry cry to be fed, the homeless to be housed. We live in the midst of a world in need of peace and a people in need of hope.**

Leader: We are gathered for worship.

People:      **There is much to do in our lives. There are commitments to fulfill, jobs to do. We must care for our children, our parents, our homes.**

Leader:      We are gathered for worship.

People:      **The problems of this world call for energy and vision.**

Leader:      In worship we seek God's vision of hope and wholeness and meet the Spirit who gives strength to the weary.

People:      **The demands of our lives call for patience and compassion.**

Leader:      In worship our spirits are renewed by God's grace and our hearts are made wide by God's love.

People:      **We have gathered for worship.**

Leader:      Come, let us worship God in this hour that we may live as God's people in days to come.

✝✝✝

Leader:      Grace and peace to you in the name of our God, the maker of all things, the One who knit our very beings together.

People:      **We come to worship this God, whose greatness is beyond our power to fully know, and yet who knows us right well.**

**We come to worship the God who knows not only the farthest reaches of the galaxy, but also the hidden places of our hearts.**

Leader:      Grace and peace to you in the name of our Lord Jesus Christ.

People:      **We gather to worship in the name of this Christ who walked among us, bringing God's word of love to all who were forgotten, God's word of grace to all who were broken, and God's word of life to all who face death.**

**We worship in Christ's name that we might live as his people.**

Leader:    Grace and peace to you, by the living power of the Holy Spirit, moving in our midst to inspire and to guide, to bring forth new life wherever it may be found.

People:    **As we worship, we open our hearts and our lives to this Spirit, that we may choose wisely, live rightly, and serve compassionately.**
**We wait for this Spirit, for there is much within us waiting to be born.**

✝✝✝

Leader:    Worship is a gift from God.

People:    **In worship, we are invited to come into the very presence of God, to be met by God's grace and encircled by God's love.**

Leader:    Worship is a promise.

People:    **In worship, we see the vision of the day yet to come, the hope of what is yet to be. In this present hour we wait for the coming kingdom.**

Leader:    Worship is demand.

People:    **In worship, God demands from us the best of our heads and our hearts. God demands of us our very lives.**

Leader:    With gratitude and joy, promise and hope, commitment and dedication, let us worship the Lord our God.

✝✝✝

Leader:    God of all Creation,

People:    **God of this present hour,**

All:       **We lift our voices in praise.**

Leader:    We praise You with voices rich in gladness and joy.

People:    **We praise You with voices hoarse with questions.**

| | |
|---|---|
| Leader: | We praise You with voices soft with worry. |
| **People:** | **We praise You with all that we are.** |
| **All:** | **We trust You for all that we hope to be.** |

✝✝✝

| | |
|---|---|
| Leader: | This is the day that the Lord has made, let us rejoice and be glad in it. |
| **People:** | **Like Miriam, let us sing with gladness, for our God triumphs over evil and oppression.** |
| Leader: | Like Hannah, let us pray with grateful hearts, for the Lord our God hears our prayer. |
| **People:** | **Like Jacob, let us wrestle with God, for out of such struggles new faith is born.** |
| Leader: | Like Abraham, let us respond to God's calling, for in faith's journey we find our lives. |
| **People:** | **This is the day that the Lord has made, let us rejoice and be glad in it.** |

✝✝✝

| | |
|---|---|
| Leader: | We are gathered for worship. |
| **People:** | **In a world of half-truths, we need a time of truth-telling.** |
| Leader: | In a world of many gods, we need an encounter with the one true God. |
| **People:** | **In a world that demands so much—and yet so little of us—we need to be confronted with a gospel that will ask of us our very lives.** |
| Leader: | In the name of God, we gather for worship today. |

✝✝✝

Leader: May the God of all grace and compassion be present among us as we worship this day.

People: **Listening for the voice of God, may we also hear the cries of our brothers and sisters in need.**

Leader: Seeking God's healing love in our lives,

People: **May we also feel the pain of those whose hurts are uncared for.**

Leader: Lifting our songs of praise and thanksgiving,

People: **May we also offer to God our lives, dedicated to living out the gospel of peace.**

Leader: God, be with us in our worship

People: **Lest in shutting the doors of this sanctuary we also shut the doors of our hearts.**

Leader: Lest we believe that in closing our eyes to pray, we can close our eyes to a world in need.

People: **God be with us.**

✝✝✝

Leader: We gather together for worship, singing our praises.

People: **Some sing gladly, joyfully, for there is much to celebrate.**

Leader: Some sing quietly, nourished by a deep and inner peace.

People: **Some sing haltingly, their notes tripping over their fears.**

Leader: Some sing longingly, remembering good days past, not yet daring to hope for the days to come.

People: **Accept, O Lord, our worship, and by Your loving presence weave our many melodies into one great symphony of devotion.**

✝✝✝

# Invocations

For every pilgrim searching for a home,
    for every son or daughter seeking a family,
    for every weary soul longing for rest
       and hurting heart aching for healing,
    for every person who seeks more challenge,
      more meaning,
          a deeper kind of life than merely existing,
For all of us,
    may this be a place of healing and homecoming.
In this hour,
    may the seekers be found by You.
      For You are our life and our hope.
                Amen.

✝✝✝

    In the midst of our praise,
      be Thou our joy.
    In the midst of our doubt,
      be Thou our faith.
    In the midst of our despair,
      be Thou our hope.
    In the midst of our fear,
      be Thou our strength.
    In the midst of our worship,
      be Thou present.
      Amen.

✝✝✝

God of all glory and of all grace,
As You receive our praise, hear our prayer. Let our adoration be
not merely lip-service, but go heart-deep. May our prayers be not
shopping lists of wants but conversations grounded in commitment. May our faith be not confined to this time and this place,
but be woven into the very fabric of our lives.
    By faith, may we hear Your voice.
    By grace, may we answer Your call.
    Amen.


                            †††


Loving God,
We are afraid.
In a world obsessed with youth,
    we are afraid of growing old.
In the midst of the city,
    we are afraid of being alone.
In a society fascinated by fantasy,
    we are afraid of the demands of reality.
In an age torn by war,
    we are afraid of the demands of peace.
Help us to come this morning bringing our fears.
Grant us courage to expose them to the light of your Presence.
Make us ready to accept the demands of your will.
For in your love is peace that goes beyond all fear.
                            Amen.


                            †††


Ever-present God,
    stir in our hearts a holy expectancy
    so that we will be ready and open
        to hear your voice.

May our spirit be open to the calling of your Spirit,
   That in listening for you we might hear you,
   that in waiting for you we might meet you,
   that in meeting you we might follow you.
                Amen.

✝✝✝

We have taught ourselves well, O Lord, how to act like adults in worship. But let us not forget that we are also your children.
And so, like children running to the safe arms of a loving parent,
   we come to you . . .
      bringing our skinned egos and bruised hearts,
      bringing the darkness of our fears into your light,
      seeking your wisdom,
         your encouraging,
            accepting grace
               that gives us strength to face the world.
And like children,
   we bring our love to you,
      offering it unashamedly,
         unreservedly.
         Amen.

✝✝✝

God of our fathers and of our mothers,
   we come to worship this day with the deep and stubborn hope that You will be our God as well. We pray that as we worship that we, too, will find our calling, our hope, our strength. In many and various ways You have spoken to our fathers and our mothers. Speak now to us.
   For we are waiting, we are listening, we are longing
      to be Your people in this time and in this place. Amen.

Loving God,
    Calm the frantic beatings of our hearts,
    smooth the wrinkled lines of our brow.
May we be still and open to the holiness of your peace,
    and the peace of your holiness.
We come together as your people,
    unfinished and unsure,
        sinners in need of grace . . .
but also children of grace ready to sing your praise.
May we worship and serve
   in your name.
        Amen.

✝✝✝

O God whose love will not let us go,
    for the sake of that love we gather together to worship you.
Because we have known your love in creation,
    we give you praise.
Because your love has sustained us,
    we give you thanks.
Because your love calls us to be more
    than we could ever be alone,
        we seek your will.
Guard our hearts, lest we think that our love for you can be
confined to this one day and this one place.
    Guard our hearts, lest we think that our love for you can be
divorced from the way that we love one another.
Open our eyes.
Empower our hearts
   as we worship this day.
        Amen.

✝✝✝

God of light,
    God of grace,
        God of peace,
In our worship we seek the light of Your presence.
We seek it, and yet would turn away from it, for you may illuminate more than it is comfortable for us to see. We may see the dust and dirt of guilt that clings so closely to us. We may see the walls that we have built so cleverly between ourselves . . . and You.
    Still, we long for Your Spirit moving in our worship.
        By Your grace, O Lord, wash us and make us clean.
        By Your love, O Lord, tear down our walls,
            build up our lives.
                Amen.

†††

Lord our God,
    with half-remembered hopes,
        half-forgotten dreams . . .
    with newly-discovered joy,
        and ancient pain . . .
    with purpose and resolve,
        and with questions and doubts,
            we come from the heat of our days
            seeking the cool of your presence.
Come, Holy Spirit, and fill our worship
    lest we forget our past,
    lest we be too satisfied with our present,
    lest we be too casual about our future.
By our worship,
    strengthen our commitment,
    renew our vision,
    deepen our faith.
Hear this prayer, O Lord, from your people.
Hear this prayer, O Lord, to be your people.
        Amen.

God of infinite love and particular compassion,
 who loves all of us and each of us,
  we thank you for the gift of this moment,
and we offer it to you as a gift of praise,
 of gratitude,
  of worship.
We come bringing a patchwork quilt of hopes and fears to this worship, all bound together by the stubborn belief that what we do in this place and in this hour may make a difference in the rest of our lives.
 And so we offer this worship to you,
  wanting to believe,
   daring to believe that you would speak,
    even to the likes of us.
May the fresh wind of your Spirit blow through this worship so that we might know your Presence.
 More we cannot ask.
 Less we cannot bear.
     Amen.

     †††

O Lord our God,
 You who are Truth, be in our worship today.
Open our eyes and ears to the truth of your gospel,
that it might confront us,
 challenge us,
  comfort us.
You who are Spirit, be in our worship today.
Provoke our praise, inspire our prayers, move our hearts,
 our minds,
  our wills.
Almighty God,
 teach us how to worship you in Spirit and in Truth.
  In the name of Jesus Christ,
   the Way, the Truth, and the Life,
    we pray.
     Amen.

May our thanksgiving be not merely routine,
    but spring from the deep, glad places of our hearts.
May our prayers and words and songs ring with the honesty of
confession, the warmth of love,
    the stubbornness of hope.
 Open our eyes to the holiness that is around us. Open our hearts
to the God who is among us. Amen.


✝✝✝


Holy and loving God,
    We come again to gather for worship partly out of habit, but
also out of hunger. We are hungry for a deeper meaning to life
than simply paying the bills and getting through the day. We are
hungry for commitment to something greater than just ourselves
and our families. Deep down, we are hungry for Your grace that
accepts us, and Your love that will not leave us. We are hungry for
Your Presence that heals our broken places and fills up our empty
places, and touches our lives with gentle hope.
    Only You can fill the deep places of our hearts.
    Be Thou with us.
        Amen.


✝✝✝


God of our worship,
    Lord of our Life,
We offer all that we are to You in worship.
Where we are strong, bless our strength. Where we are wounded,
heal us. Where we are weary, revive and renew us. We bring to
You all that we are—the strong and the weak, the light and the
dark, the good and the evil, and trust in Your accepting grace.
Accept this our worship, O Lord, and be Thou present in the midst
of it. Amen.

God of love,
> God of life,

We open our hearts to You in worship this morning. May Your grace heal our hearts. May Your peace calm our fears. May the fresh wind of Your Spirit fan into flame the sparks of joy that lie within us.

We confess, O Lord, that we don't always know how to live with You. But we know that we cannot live without You.

Hear our prayers that we speak and sing,
> and hear the cries of our Spirit that are too deep for words.

Be Thou known to us in the breaking of bread.
Be Thou known to us in the living of our lives.
> Amen.

✝✝✝

Lord our God,
> Sharpen our vision and adjust our focus
>> lest we mistake small things for great,
> lest we confuse the temporary with the eternal,

lest we believe that faith
> is a matter of having all of the right answers.

Be Thou present to make of this time a holy time.
Amen.

✝✝✝

Lord of all life,
keeper and sustainer of all of us . . .
> and of each of us,
>> come, and guide our worship.

Lest we be lulled into thinking that worship is mostly a task to be done rather than a Presence to be entered into.

 Grant to us the grace to open out hearts to Your love.
> Grant to us the courage to open our ears to Your Word.

We are Your people, O Lord.
Do with us what You will,
> for in your will is our life, our joy, our peace. Amen.

In You, O God, is our hope.
In You is our strength.
    And so we worship You.
    And so we seek You.
May our restless spirits find their rest in You.
May our hurting Spirits find their balm in You.
May our hungering spirits find in You
    their strength,
    their sustenance.
May we who seek, find.
May we who hunger, be filled.
    Amen.


✝✝✝


Almighty God,
    You are the cause for our celebration,
    our reason for worship,
    our strength for the present and our hope for the future.
But sometimes, O Lord,
    You are the disturber of our souls.
Trouble the waters deep within us that we may be healed
    of old ways of thinking,
    of old ways of seeing our world,
    of old ways of living.
For we are Your children, O God,
    and we are called to be new creations.
        In the name of Christ our Lord, we pray.
        Amen.


✝✝✝


God whose love is never ending,
    whose grace is never-failing,
        we come gladly into Your Presence,
To praise You with our songs
    and to thank You with our prayers.

We come together
>to seek You with all of our minds,
>to love You with all of our hearts,
>to follow You with all that we are.

Help us to worship not for any hope of gain
>or prize to be earned,
>>but because we are Your children.

You have loved us,
>You have called us by name.
>>And that is enough.
>>>Amen.

✝✝✝

God who has created the heavens and the earth,
>and who has known us before we came to be,
>>we gather again to worship You.

Some of us come because it is a holy habit that gives meaning to our days. Some of us come because joy must be shared and thanks must be given. Some of us come hoping against hope to find strength for hard days ahead. Some of us come slightly bored—not only with this routine but with life itself.

We come to You, O God,
>and ask for Your presence among us.

For only You can speak to all of us—
>and to each of us.

Only You can take our jumbled threads and weave them into a great tapestry of faith.
>By Your Spirit, O God, be with us. Amen.

✝✝✝

Loving God,
Be with us in our worship that we might learn
   the sound of Your voice,
   the warmth of Your presence,
   the light of Your love,
   the sound of Your calling.
May we listen and learn of these things in the calm and quiet of this place, so that we might know them in times of noise and hurriedness and confusion. Let us know You here, O God, so that we might recognize You when we meet You elsewhere.
   May we serve You by worshiping You,
      and worship You by serving You.
         Amen.


                              †††


O Lord our God,
In the midst of friends and family,
   you come as a stranger seeking welcome.
In the midst of the practical and pragmatic matters of our lives,
   You come as a dreamer pointing to a greater vision.
In the midst of our questions,
   You come as a sure and solid rock,
 and in the midst of our too-glib answers
   You come as a troubling question.
In the midst of ordinary people in an ordinary town
   on an ordinary corner,
      You come as the Holy One.
And in the midst of the pomp and pageantry of the world,
   You come as a simple child.
We cannot pin You down, O Lord. We cannot box You in. But grant to us the courage and the grace to welcome You as You come in our midst. Amen.


                              †††

God of the heavens and the earth,
    God of all creation and God of our lives.
We come as strangers and we come as friends.
    We come with our hurts and we come with our hopes.
We come with our fears and we come with our dreams.
    We come with our faith and we come with our doubts.
We have gathered for worship, O Lord,
    with hearts sometimes divided and minds sometimes
        distracted.
But this we know,
    unless You be present, our worship will be in vain.
And if You be present,
    all shall be well.
Come, O Lord, and grace our worship—
    and our lives—
        with Your presence. Amen.

✝✝✝

Hear us, O Lord, as we pray.
As the rains have refreshed the earth,
    may your Spirit refresh the dry and thirsty places
        within us.
As we celebrate this young life among us,
    may we be open to the birth of new life within us.
As we come to worship,
    may we be met by the One who loved us
        even before we came to be,
            whose love redeems our past,
            safeguards our future,
            and surrounds us this very day.
God of all hope,
    all life,
        for this we pray.
            Amen.

✝✝✝

God who is our light and our life,
We gather again for worship knowing deep within us that in
the midst of things to be done and tasks to be accomplished, we
need this time of patient waiting upon Your presence. In the midst
of all of the words said to us and about us, we need to listen to
Your Word. In the midst of a world and a culture that would
shape us and bend us and mold us into its image, we need to be
reminded of who we are . . . and of whose we are.
We are created in Your image, O God. And we are Your children. Fill our worship with Your presence that our lives might be
filled by Your grace. Amen.


☩☩☩


God of wonder that goes beyond words,
God of hope that goes beyond fears,
    all that hath life and breath come now to praise You.
And all who seek life—
    life that is more than mere breath,
    life that springs from deep places,
    life that is filled by Your grace
        and graced by Your love,
            come now to seek You—
                giver of all life,
                giver of life's meaning.
Meet us here, O Lord, as we worship together. Amen.


☩☩☩


God whose Spirit has cut across our lines of race and class,
    age and gender
        to create one new people,
    we, Your people, have gathered for worship.
Open our ears and eyes and hearts

to the Presence of Your Spirit among us
that we might have the courage and vision to be the Church,
gathered for worship,
scattered through the world,
That we might believe
that what can happen in this hour
might be life-changing,
life-giving.
We are more than a group of people gathered for a meeting;
we are the body of Christ,
daring to worship.
By Your Spirit, O Lord,
remind us of who we are,
lest we forget. Amen.


✝✝✝


Holy and loving God,
You who created the world and all that is in it,
who sustains the universe and all that is beyond it,
You are beyond our knowing.
We cannot understand You completely.
We cannot comprehend the breadth and depth
of Your power and your love.
And yet,
You have chosen to be among us,
to walk with us,
to love us,
to die for us.
May the warmth of Your love
chase away the cold chill of our fears.
May the fire of Your love
burn away all that is false within us.
May the light of Your love
shine throughout our worship and our lives.
Amen.

Immortal, invisible You are, O God,
    clothed in the light of Your glory,
    the splendor of Your majesty.
And yet You have chosen to reach across the holy distance
 to welcome us,
 to accept us,
    to love us,
        to save us.
Lest we treat this uncommon gospel as common news,
    be Thou present.
Lest in our logical and practical lives,
    we lose sight of wonder and mystery,
        be Thou present.
Lest we treat faith too lightly,
        prayer too glibly,
            discipleship too comfortably,
                be Thou present.
                    Amen.


                    †††


God who is our Creator, Redeemer, and Lord,
    We gather again for worship.
We gather to meet the Lord whose name we bear. We gather to
seek the presence of the God who formed and fashioned us. We
gather to wait upon the Spirit that both strengthens and sustains
us.
    In a world of petty dreams,
        we seek a great vision.
    In a world of empty conversation,
        we seek a living Word.
O God, we are your people.
Be Thou with us. Amen.


                    †††

Love that has known us before we were yet born,
Love that has sustained us through all of our days,
Love that will not let us go,
    O God of Love,
        we come to worship You.
As we worship,
      give to us eyes to see you at work in this world.
Give to us ears to hear your calling,
    and hearts brave enough to love you—
       and our neighbors.
Give to us minds willing to be shaped by the mind of Christ
that our lives might reflect the light of your presence. Amen.


✝✝✝


Lord our God,
    who is higher than the heavens
    and yet closer than our very breath,
     hear our prayer.
May we give to you of our best—
    the best of our minds . . .
        open to wonder,
        willing to question,
        eager for fresh new directions of your Spirit.
May we give you the best of our hearts . . .
    our first love,
    our deepest commitment.
As we worship you, O Lord,
    may we give you our best.
        Amen.


✝✝✝

God who has created all things
   and who has loved all of creation,
      we have gathered to worship you.
Hear our prayers, O Lord.
Hear the prayers of hearts overflowing with gladness.
Hear the quiet prayers whispered in gentle faith.
Hear the stuttering prayers of those who doubt,
   and the clenched-teeth prayers of those who hurt.
Hear our prayers, O Lord,
   and in this hour of worship speak to us.
Let us give thanks for what has been.
Let us yet hope for what shall be.
In the name of Jesus Christ our Lord, we pray.
Amen.

✝✝✝

O God most holy and most near,
As we worship you
   grant to us new eyes to see the world as you see it.
Grant to us new ears
   to hear the startling news of your gospel.
Grant to us new hearts
   to love you unashamedly
   and to love our brothers and sisters unreservedly.
Grant to us new hands
   to do the work of the kingdom,
      to bind up the wounded,
      to set free the captives,
      to welcome the stranger.
As we worship, O Lord,
   make of us a new creation. Amen.

✝✝✝

Almighty God,
In the midst of the chatter of our days,
    may we make a space for silences.
In the midst of all of the doings of our week,
    may we make a space for stillness.
In the midst of our pragmatic plans and programs,
    may we make a space in our lives for worship—
        nothing more and nothing less than worship.
For only by your Presence may the deep places of our hearts be
touched. Only in your light do we see who we really are.
In the name of Jesus Christ our Lord, we pray. Amen.


†††


O Lord our God,
    Creator, Redeemer, Sustainer of all life,
Open our eyes that we might see
    the everyday glory around us.
Open our ears
    that we might hear the sounds of creation's praise.
As we worship,
    let us seek not to drown them out,
    but rather to sing in harmony with all that You have made.
May our worship and our lives
    join with creation's hymn of praise. Amen.


†††

# Litanies and Responsive Readings

| | |
|---|---|
| Leader: | Beloved, let us love one another, for love is of God, and the person who loves is born of God and knows God. |
| People: | **I was hungry, and you gave me food. I was thirsty, and you gave me drink.** |
| Leader: | But if anyone has the world's goods and sees his brother or sister in need, yet closes his heart, how does God's love abide in that person? |
| People: | **I was a stranger and you welcomed me. I was naked and you clothed me.** |
| Leader: | In this the love of God was made manifest among us, that God sent God's only Son into the world so that we might live through him. . . . If God so loved us, we ought to love one another. |
| People: | **Let us love not in word and speech but in deed and in truth.** |
| All: | **And Jesus said, "As you did it to the least of these, you did it unto me."** |

†††

| | |
|---|---|
| Leader: | "And it shall come to pass afterward, that I shall pour out my Spirit on all flesh. Your sons and Your daughters shall prophecy. . . ." |
| People: | **"There is neither Jew nor Greek. . . ."** |
| Leader: | "Your old men shall dream dreams and your young men shall see visions. . . ." |
| People: | **"There is neither slave nor free. . . ."** |
| Leader: | "Even upon the menservants and the maidservants I will pour out my spirit." |
| People: | **"There is neither male nor female; for you are all one in Christ Jesus."** |

*(Moment of Silence)*

Leader: Renew within us, O Lord, a vision of Your kingdom, where the last shall be first and the first shall be last.

People: **And all of our neat and ancient walls of division are broken down by the fresh wind of Your Spirit.**

Leader: Renew within us, O Lord, a vision of Your kingdom, where the greatest ones are those who serve,

People: **And all of our gifts are blessed, not by the power that we wield, but by the grace by which we are called.**

All: **Amen.**

††††

Leader: For freedom, Christ has set us free. . . .

People: **We have been set free from our old way of life.**

Leader: From pride that blinds us to our own sin and from prejudice that blinds us to our neighbor's needs.

People: **From envy that resents that someone else has more than we have, and from greed that declares that we never have enough.**

Leader: For freedom, Christ has set us free. . . .

People: **We have been set free from serving things that do not last and power that is ultimately powerless. We have been set free to serve the living God of our salvation.**

Leader: In giving up our lives, we find them. In becoming slaves, we are set free.

††††

Leader: "On the day of Pentecost, they gathered in Jerusalem. And the Holy Spirit came upon them.

People: **"Now there were dwelling in Jerusalem Jews, devout persons from every nation under heaven.**

Leader:   "And at the sound, the multitude came together, and they were bewildered, because everyone heard them speaking in their own language.

People:   **"And they were amazed and wondered, saying, 'Are not all these who are speaking Galilean? And how is it that we hear each of us in our native language?' "**

Leader:   We, too, have gathered from different places. We, too, speak different languages.

People:   **Some of us speak the language of hope; others speak the language of despair.**

Leader:   Some speak the language of encouragement; others speak the language of doubt.

People:   **Some speak the language of pain; others speak the language of healing.**

Leader:   Some speak the language of weariness; others speak the language of strength.

People:   **May we, as we meet together, hear and understand one another's language.**

Leader:   For we are all sisters and brothers, and together speak the language of faith.

†††

Leader:   For the gift of dreams and visions, we thank You, O Lord.

People:   **For the vision of people like Abraham and Sarah who go forth into unknown futures and unknown places, the assurance of God's call their only security, we give You thanks.**

Leader:   For the vision of people like Jeremiah who proclaim God's word in difficult times as well as good, we give You thanks.

People:   **For the vision of people like Anna and Simeon who in patience and faith wait for the fulfillment of the vision, we give You thanks.**

Leader: For the vision of people like Paul who break down old boundaries of faith that divide rather than unite, we give You thanks.

**People: For the vision of people like Phoebe who serve with quiet and constant faithfulness, we give You thanks.**

Leader: For the vision of God's people throughout the ages that has withstood persecution and trial, that has been open to the ever-blowing fresh wind of the Spirit, we give You thanks.

**People: May our vision and dream be guided by Your Spirit, bringing vision to the young and dreams to the old,**

Leader: Leading Your daughters and Your sons to proclaim Your message.

**People: May our dream and vision be guided by Your vision . . . to preach good news to the poor,**

Leader: To proclaim release to the captives and recovery of sight to the blind,

**People: To set at liberty those who are oppressed.**

**All: May Your dream, O Lord, be our dream.**

✝✝✝

## *Litany of Memory*

Leader: We gather together this day to remember our family and friends who have died in this past year. We remember them. . . . (*Names are read aloud*)

**People: We give you thanks, O God, for those whom we have loved. We give you thanks for the laughter and the love, the insight and the strength that they gave to us.**

Leader: We thank you, O Lord, for bringing into being these unique people, and for bringing them into our lives.

**People: And now their death has left an empty place within us.**

Leader: So we pray for ourselves, for the days when that empty place hurts like a raw wound and for the days when it returns as a gentle ache in the midst of the everyday living of our lives.

People: **We hold onto the memory of those who have died, but we also pray for the grace to let go of any hurts unforgiven, any conflict unresolved, and words from the heart left unsaid.**

Leader: O Lord, you have promised Your presence through the valley of the shadow of death.

People: **We pray in confident trust that those who have passed through that valley are now in Your gentle arms.**
**And for we who remain on this side of the valley, we pray for strength in our grieving and joy in our remembering.**

Leader: "Therefore, since we are surrounded by so great a cloud of witnesses . . . let us run with perseverance the race that is set before us."

People: **For these, our family and friends, we give You thanks.**

✝✝✝

## Litany for the Commissioning of Workers

Leader: "Now there are varieties of gifts, but the same Spirit,

*Workers:* *"There are varieties of service, but the same Lord,*

Leader: "There are varieties of working, but it is the same God who inspires them all in every one." (1 Cor 12:4-5)

*Workers:* *We thank you, O Lord, that you have created us as uniquely gifted individuals.*

Leader: "Jesus said to his disciples, 'Let the greatest among you become as the youngest, and the leader as one who serves.' " (Luke 22:26)

*Workers:* *We accept the calling of Christ to use our gifts in the service of God's kingdom through this church.*

People: **We, this church, covenant with you to support your service with our prayers and our skills. We charge you to carry out your responsibilities with faith, hope, and**

most of all, love . . . for the Lord our God, for your
sisters and brothers in faith, and for this part of the
body of Christ.

*Workers:*   *By God's grace, we will.*

†††

## *Litany for the Dedication of Instruments*

Leader:     "The Lord is my strength and my song." (Exodus 15:2)
People:     **"The Lord is my strength and my shield; in God my
            heart trusts; so I am helped and my heart exults, and
            with my song give thanks to the Lord." (Psalm 28:7)**
Leader:     We thank You, O Lord, for this gift of music.
People:     **The music by which we praise You and give thanks.**
Leader:     On this day, we dedicate to You the music of this ___.
People:     **May the music that it brings to us always be a
            reminder of Your love and grace.**
Leader:     May we use it faithfully, for Your honor and Your
            glory.
People:     **Bless, O Lord, this gift of music.**
Leader:     Bless those whose commitment and gifts bring the
            notes to life.
People:     **And bless those who will receive this offering of music.**
Leader:     May our worship be inspired,
People:     **And our service strengthened,**
Leader:     For we worship and serve in the name of the Lord, our
            strength and our song.
All:        **Amen.**

†††

# Prayers

## Prayers of Confession

O God of the ages and of this present hour,
  hear our prayer and forgive our sins.
We confess that we have hoarded our love, giving but the smallest
portion. We confess, O God, that we have not always loved our
neighbors as we ought. Too easily we grow impatient with them,
too easily we dismiss them, too easily we turn a deaf ear to them.
Forgive us.
  We confess, O God, that we have not always loved ourselves
as we ought. Too quickly we give up on ourselves, and too long
we remember our failures. We try to be more—and less—than You
created us to be. Forgive us.
  We confess, O God, that we have not always loved You as we
ought. We have hid from You in our shame; we have ignored You
in our indifference. Too often we run here and there trying to give
You everything except that which You most desire—our love.
Forgive us. Free us, O Lord, to love you with all that we are and
to love our neighbors as ourselves. Amen.

†††

O Lord our God, forgive us.
We want answers that are easy,
    roads that are smooth,
    results that are quick.
Like spoiled children we want our way—now.
We want one key that will unlock all doors,
    one elixir that will cure all ills,
    one solution that will cure all problems.
And somewhere in all of our searchings,
    You are left behind.
We confess that we have traded reality for illusion,
            vision for blindness,
            wisdom for foolishness.

Forgive us.
Restore us.
> For we pray in the name of Christ our Lord,
> > Amen.


✝✝✝


Forgive us, O Lord.
We have spoken when it was a time for silence.
We have acted when it was a time to wait.
And when You have called us to speak and to act, we have
remained silent and still.
> Forgive us, O Lord. Amen.


✝✝✝


God of compassion.
> if our thanksgiving is no more than self-congratulation,
> if we pray but do not give,
> if we do not see You among persons of all races,
> > > and ages,
> > > and economic resources,

Forgive us.
Grant to us a spirit of gratitude
> that opens our hands
> > and our hearts. Amen.


✝✝✝


Loving God,
You made us free.
Yet we prefer slavery, for slaves don't have choices.

Deciding is difficult, for it's never between right and wrong,
    but good or better
        bad or worse.
In a gray world we cry for lines of black and white.
God, forgive us,
   for we have made Your blessing into a curse,
     Your gift into a burden.
We confess that we'd like to stay children.
Forgive us. Amen.

✝✝✝

For our lack of faith
   that fills each day with tension and worry,
For our lack of hope
   that clouds our future with despair and anxiety,
For our lack of love
   that fails to place You at the center of our lives,
O Lord,
   forgive us. Amen.

✝✝✝

God of the ages and of this present moment,
   forgive us.
We confess that too often we live by tunnel vision,
   failing to see beyond tomorrow's deadline.
We become immersed in our little worlds, and let an entire world
pass by, unnoticed and unloved.
   Frustration overcomes patience, and anxiety replaces faith.
   Your promises come easily to our lips,
     but are more difficult in our lives.
We confess our sins, O Lord, asking that in Your forgiveness we
receive a wider vision, a sense of history and future much larger
than our tiny moment in time.
 Grant to us faith to accept Your Word,
   and hope that comes from its presence in our lives. Amen.

Lord, forgive us. We come to worship You, but feel no awe. We sing Your praises, but feel no joy. We confess our sins, but are not truly repentant. We declare Your message, but feel no responsibility.

Jolt us out of our comfortable sleep with the sharp cries of the lost, the needy, the suffering. Break down our ivory towers with the hard stones of reality. Forgive us the sin of our complacency.

Lord, hear our prayer, for in Your forgiveness, we are healed.

Amen.

†††

Holy God,

we confess that we are the ones who have done so little with so much. We have neglected our opportunities, wasted our resources, and treated Your grace as the just reward for our labors. God, forgive us, for we have separated gratitude and responsibility. Our thanksgiving has become a tribute to our own cleverness. Forgive us the hardness of our hearts and the smallness of our vision.

Amen.

†††

Almighty God,

We come seeking Your forgiveness.

You have spoken, but we have not listened.

You have commanded, but we have not acted.

You have called, but we have not followed.

We have loved our comfort more than we have loved Your will.

Forgive us, O Lord. Amen.

†††

God of all life and of all hope,
We confess that we come together bringing with us handfuls of
fear and superstition. We are afraid of the world around us, and
of the person inside us. We are looking for a good luck charm, a
reward for ritual dutifully completed.

Strip away our masks, O Lord. Collect the scenery that we so
carefully construct to fool our friends, our families, ourselves . . .
and You. Leave us not broken but whole, not anxious but calm. In
this time may we catch a glimpse of who we really are, and by
Your grace, who we may become. Amen.

††† 

Lord God,
If we fail to see the explosion of color around us,
If we never stop to feel the sun on our faces,
If we neglect to listen to the music of birds
    and the laughter of children,
        forgive us.
Open our hearts to the grace and truth
    that surrounds and fills the ordinary days of our lives.
Remind us of how You made
 the common
        uncommon. Amen.

††† 

Our God,
    forgive us. We try to save the world by ourselves, ending up
only tired and frustrated. We try to do everything, even that which
You have not called us to do. Busy and fatigued and impatient, we
are unable to respond when You do call us to action, for our

schedules have become our excuses. Yet our pride keeps us from Your rest and refreshment and guidance.

Forgive us, O Lord, and help us to see the good we should do, the time we should rest, the way that we should trust. Grant to us endurance, patience, and wisdom. Amen.

✝✝✝

Forgive us O Lord, for we have sinned.
We have seen the gospel through the eyes of the world,
     instead of seeing the world through the eyes of the gospel.
We have sought the easy way rather than Your way.
Forgive us, O Lord, we pray. Amen.

✝✝✝

God of grace and glory,
     You have called us to great visions. But we confess that too often we have let petty matters sidetrack great dreams. Forgive us when we are so preoccupied by the trivial that we lose sight of the eternal.

You have called us to be brothers and sisters. But we confess that too often we find it easier to find fault than to offer grace. Forgive us when we are more interested in how we will look to one another than in how we will live together.

You have called us to be salt and light. But we confess that too often we have been content to be pale imitations that neither cause a ripple nor make a difference. Forgive us when we would rather go along with this world than risk challenging this world. Amen.

✝✝✝

Forgive us, O Lord, for we have sinned.
We have trusted in our strength
  rather than Your power.
We have trusted in our cleverness
  rather than in Your wisdom.
We have trusted in our deeds
  rather than Your grace.
      Merciful God, forgive us.
      Amen.


††† 


Forgive us, O Lord, for we have sinned.
You have called us to confession, but we'd rather offer excuses. You have called us to live as new creations in the new world of your kingdom, but still we cling to the security of old lives and familiar lands. Your call is difficult and challenging, and we confess, O Lord, that it is hard to hear . . . and follow.

   And yet, only in your love are we made whole.
   Only in your life do we find our lives.
   Only by following you
      can we be all that we were created to be.
   Forgive us, O Lord, and open our ears to hear your calling, our hearts to receive your grace. Amen.


††† 


Merciful God,
   hear our prayer.
   Forgive us, for we've not always known what to do with this matter of faith. We leave it behind on Sunday morning, like a forgotten umbrella left on a pew. We encase it in glass and mark it as fragile lest it get scratched, broken, or bruised. We display it on a table where it may be seen but will not be in the way.

Forgive us, O God, for choosing to protect our faith rather than live it, to admire it rather than to be molded by it. Forgive us, O God, when we cling to a faith too small for the challenge of this life and the hope of the life to come.

Forgive us, and renew within us a great and living faith.
Amen.

†††

Forgive us, O God, for we take ourselves too seriously.
Wrapped up in ourselves,
we forget how to laugh,
to celebrate,
to dance.
In trying so hard to be grown up, we forget how to play.
Neglecting Your gift of belly laughs and joy, our lives grow stale and tired.

Forgive us, O Lord, and, at least once in a while, grant to us the grace of giggles. Amen.

†††

God who is the creator of heaven and earth,
and the sustainer of all life,
we confess our sin to You.
You have given us
the extraordinary gift of life,
yet we treat it as a common and ordinary thing.
You have promised us
Your presence in all times and all places of our lives,
and yet we casually stroll over holy ground,
unthinking and unmoved.
You are the Word in our midst,
but we are so full of the chatter of our own lives
that we do not hear You.

Forgive us, O Lord,
    when we receive so great a mystery with indifference.
Forgive us, O Lord,
    when accomplishing our agenda becomes more important
        than dreaming Your dreams and following Your vision.
Forgive us, O Lord. Amen.

✝✝✝

When our faith becomes more duty than delight,
    O Lord,
        forgive us.
           Amen.

✝✝✝

Almighty God,
    by whose power the world came to be,
        hear our prayer,
        for we have misunderstood and misused power.
We confess that all too often we have used our power
    to silence those with whom we disagree,
    to exclude those who are different,
    and to cast out those whom we fear.
We act as if our power is a battle prize to be fought for
        and a weapon to be used.
Forgive us, Lord, for—in abusing our power—we have hurt our
brothers and sisters.
    Forgive us, O Lord,
    for we confess that at times
        we have also traded away our power too cheaply.
Like Esau, we have traded our birthrights for ease.
Rather than risking confrontation,
    we have stood idly by in the face of injustice.

We have silenced our voices, rather than risk speaking truth.
Forgive us, O Lord.
>Hear our prayer, Almighty God,
>and teach us to be good stewards,
>>not only of money and time and gifts, but also of power.
>>Amen.

†††

Leader:    I lift my eyes unto the hills—Where does my help come from?

**People:    Forgive us, O God, when we believe our only help is in our own strength.**

Leader:    My help comes from the Lord, the maker of heaven and earth.

**People:    Forgive us, O God, when we believe that our only hope is in the quickness of our own minds.**

Leader:    The Lord watches over you—
The Lord is at your right hand.

**People:    Forgive us, O God, when we believe that our future is in our hands alone.**

Leader:    The Lord will keep you from all harm; he will watch over your life.

**People:    Forgive us when we believe that we can live without Your grace.**

Leader:    The Lord will watch over your coming and your going both now and forevermore.

†††

Leader:    Great and loving God, our Creator and our Redeemer, forgive us.

**People:    For oftentimes we speak too quickly and listen half-heartedly to the heart cries of others.**

Leader:    O Lord our God, forgive us.

People: We are too easily distracted by glory that does not last and glitter that does not shine.

Leader: Ever-living God, hear our prayer.

People: We confess that we have tried to shut You up in tidy boxes of our own making, to shut You away from the mess and matter of our everyday lives.

All: Hear our prayer, O Lord, and grant to us Your grace.

## Communion Prayers

God of all time and all creation, forgive us. We are faced with a new year, but we confess that there is still much of the old still within us. We carry old hurts and anger, carefully nourished and protected. We carry old sins that have grown familiar and comfortable and safe. We carry old habits and old ways of thinking that keep You at a safe distance, for we fear that Your presence in our lives might change our lives.

Forgive us, Lord, for sometimes we'd rather hold tightly to our sins than open our hands to receive Your grace. Forgive us, O Lord, and as we share of this bread and this cup, make of us new creations. Amen.

✝✝✝

Loving God, because we are Your family, we gather here at this table. Forgive us of our sins that have divided us and isolated us from one another. As we share in this bread and this cup, may we find hope to renew our spirits, peace to heal our pain, and grace to live as Your new creations. Amen.

✝✝✝

Holy God, we gather here because we remember a night in which our Lord shared bread and a cup with his disciples. Forgive us when the familiar story becomes routine.

Help us realize the extraordinary thing that we do, for by our actions we proclaim death—and life. May we find in this meal nourishment for the living out of Your calling to be the body of Christ.

May we find here strength. May we accept grace. Amen.

✝✝✝

Almighty and loving God,

We come to this table, not because we have earned the right to be here. We come not because we have been good enough or faithful enough to deserve our place. We come because by Your grace You have welcomed us here.

Forgive us, O Lord, when we want to restrict Your invitation to those who measure up to our standards. Forgive us when we want to limit Your grace to those with whom we agree, to our friends and not to our enemies.

As we take this bread and this cup, remind us of the depth and the breadth of Your love and Your mercy. May we find here the wisdom to celebrate and live a vision of your kingdom, a kingdom whose doors are open to all who would enter in. For we pray in the name of Christ our Lord. Amen.

ttt

Forgive us, O Lord, for sometimes we are an impatient people. We seek a faith that produces immediate results. We seek a way that is quick, and quickly done with. But that is not Your way.

For You have called us to a journey measured not in moments but in lifetimes. You work in us by a slow and sometimes hidden grace. Help us to be patient, O Lord, and faithful along the way.

May this bread and this cup provide for us strength and nourishment for the long journey of faith. Amen.

## Offertory Prayers

We have received much that we did not earn . . .
    the dancing colors of spring
        and the early morning music of birds,
    the laughter of friends and the love of family,
    our very lives
    and your grace that gives our lives meaning and hope.
These things we have received as gift.
 As abundantly as we have received, let us give. Amen.

ttt

You who transformed the water into wine,
    who transformed one small meal into food sufficient for
    thousands,
we ask for your transforming power to grace these gifts.
May these ordinary gifts become extraordinary by the power of
Your love. May they become healing. May they become good
news. May they become hope. Amen.

ttt

O God,
    It is sometimes easy to speak of giving our lives to you. It is
harder to trust you with the particulars of those lives, the concrete
stuff of our days. But may we do so, for you are present in
mundane matters as well as holy moments.
    May our trust lead to obedience, and our obedience to giving.
And may our gifts become hope and light for this world. We ask
your blessing on these gifts as we pray—and give—in the name of
our Lord. Amen.

ttt

You have called us to follow you, O Lord.
May we follow you to the bedsides of those who are sick,
 to the tables of those who are hungry,
 to the prison cells of those who are captive,
 to the dark nights of those who have no hope.
We cannot be all places, O God, so bless these gifts to be your love
in all places, for all peoples.
Bless these gifts and send them to places of need.
Bless those who give,
 and send us to the places of our calling.
  Amen.

†††

May our lives reflect, O Lord, the praises that we sing.
We have received grace upon grace,
 so may we live in grace with one another.
We have received forgiveness,
 so may we forgive.
We have received gifts far beyond our need,
 so may we give.
Bless these gifts given this day and always.
Amen.

†††

Faith walks hand in hand with serving,
 and love expresses itself in giving.
May we be faithful, O Lord, in our serving
 and loving in our giving.
For we do these things in your name and asking your blessing.
Amen.

†††

May we give not out of duty,
    but out of love.
Not out of practicality,
    but with faith.
Not counting the cost, but rejoicing in the gospel. Amen.

✝✝✝

In the name of Jesus,
    we are reminded of how much we have been loved.
In the name of Jesus,
    we find the grace to love one another.
In the name of Jesus,
    we offer up this worship on this day.
In the name of Jesus,
    we give this offering of gifts
        that all peoples
            might hear this name,
            might know this Lord. Amen.

✝✝✝

Hear our prayer, O Lord.
For all good gifts,
    we give you thanks.
For all the gifts that we have wasted or neglected or abused,
    we ask your forgiveness.
For all the gifts that we offer this day,
    we ask Your blessing.
        Amen.

✝✝✝

O Creator, Redeemer, and Sustainer,
    what shall we bring to you?
Already the earth is yours.
    What shall we give to you?
Already you have given life to us.
So we give to you that which you require of us—
    our best.
We give the best of our money,
    and not simply what is left over.
We give the best of our talents,
    striving for excellence in ministry and mission.
We give the best of our heats,
    our compassion,
    our commitment,
    our love for You and one another.
Bless these gifts that we offer this hour and all the hours of our days.
    In the name of our Lord, who gave himself, we pray. Amen.

✝✝✝

By the sustaining presence of Your Spirit, O Lord, You indeed are with us.
    But You also walk among us
        as a homeless family,
        a hungry child,
        a teenager with too many tough choices to make,
    a senior adult with too few people with whom to talk,
    a man or a woman in need of hope,
        of life,
            of light.
As we give,
    may we recognize You as You walk among us.
        Amen.

✝✝✝

Above the noise of conflict,
    there is a song of peace.
Above the world's weeping,
    there is a song of hope.
Above the cries of hate,
    there is a song of love.
Bless these gifts, O Lord,
    that we, too, might be singers of Your song.
            Amen.


                        †††


God,
 our Creator, Redeemer, and friend,
Your faithfulness endures to all generations,
    from the beginning of time until all time is past.
May we, your children,
    be faithful in our time.
Accept these gifts as the expression of our faithfulness,
    and bless them for Your sake.
            Amen.


                        †††


Lord,
You have been our safety and refuge.
    But there are many who face these days not knowing
    the comfort of Your grace
        or the comfort of a home.
There are many who face these days
    not knowing the strength of Your love
        or the strength of an adequate meal.
For the sake of these,
    our brothers and sisters,
        we ask Your blessing upon this offering that we give,
        and all the gifts that we offer.
            Amen.

Grace greater than our sin,
    provision greater than our need,
        love greater than our failings.
For these things, we give thanks.
And in thanks, we return these gifts to You.
        Amen.


††† 


For all that we have received,
    may we be thankful.
For all that we hold dear,
    may we be grateful.
For all that we are called to give,
    may we answer with glad and generous hearts,
Giving in love,
    Seeking only Your blessing.
        Amen.


††† 


Some give joyfully,
    others reluctantly.
Some give out of much,
    others have little.
Some give because they have caught sight of a vision—
    or a vision has caught sight of them.
These are our gifts, O God,
    given for reasons both noble and ordinary.
Accept them.
Bless them.
Use them for Your glory and honor.
        Amen.

Beautiful is the story,
Beautiful is the light that has shined upon us.
     The people of this world need beautiful stories,
          need light,
          need life.
So we ask You to bless these gifts,
     that the story might be told,
     that the light might shine,
     that all of the peoples of this earth
          might have life. Amen.

✝✝✝

Christ whose glory fills the skies,
     may Your glory also fill the earth.
For the sake of all of the places
     where darkness and confusion still reign,
          we give.
For the sake of our own lives,
     where faith, doubt, and indifference mingle together,
          we give.
We give,
     and as we give we pray
     that opened hands be joined with open hearts.
In the name of Christ, our Lord, our Light, and our Life,
     we pray. Amen.

✝✝✝

Let us praise Thee, O God,
     not just with our voices,
          but with our actions.
Not just with our hearts
     but with our hands.
Even by our giving, may we praise Thee, O God.
Accept these gifts and use them for Your glory. Amen.

✝✝✝

## Pastoral Prayers

God in whom our lives find meaning,
  by whom our lives are sustained,
    We offer to You our praise and thanksgiving, for You alone are the Creator of the universe. Before this world existed, You were God. Before time began, You were God. And we confess that such greatness is beyond our knowing. But You have chosen to know us. To call us by name. To love us and care for us. To become as we are. To suffer the pain that we feel. It is a wonder and a mystery, and while we cannot profess to understand it all, we do give thanks for Your grace.

But there are some for whom the mystery of life has turned dark and threatening. There are those who wonder why, in a world able to sustain us all, they must go hungry. There are those who are locked into a prison of poverty, and they wonder how they will ever escape. There are those who suffer—those who suffer from illness, those who suffer in body and spirit, those who suffer the cold pangs of fear and the persistent pain of worry. There are those who suffer the agony of questions that have no answers. For these we pray.

And we confess, O Lord, that sometimes we have tried to offer answers that were too easy rather than live with the uncertainty of questions. Forgive us when we try to reduce You to something more manageable than mysterious. Forgive us when we try to fit You into our lives rather than finding our lives in You.

We pray in the name of Christ our Lord. Amen.

✝✝✝

O Lord our God, who brought light out of darkness,
  creation out of confusion,
    life out of death,
      You alone are God.
In the midst of all that calls for our attention, You alone call us by name. In the midst of everything and everyone that demands that we earn our worth and pull our weight, You offer to us grace and rest from our labors.

We confess, O God, that we are reluctant to hear Your call. For if we listen, what will You ask of us? Where will You lead us? And we confess that we are oftentimes reluctant to trust in Your grace, for the good news seems too good to be true. Who are we, that You should love us so much? Our guilt and our pride shuts the windows of our hearts, lest Your forgiving word enter and we be changed. Forgive us, O Lord.

There are those folk who have never known a word of grace, a moment of acceptance. The worker whose work is never quite good enough. The student who can never quite make the grade in the classroom or on the playing field or in the social scene. The people who stumble and bumble through life with egos forever bruised. Those who keep themselves locked in the dark prisons of their own making, their failures becoming their cell. For all who have never felt Your forgiving touch and for those who have turned it away, we pray.

We thank You, O God, for hearing our prayers, whether they be words spoken in worship or whispered in our hearts. Amen.

ttt

God of all time and space, of holy days and ordinary moments, we come to You in this time of worship.

We give You thanks for Your gift of time; for our gift of years, however many they may be, and our gift of days, whatever they may bring.

We confess, O Lord, that we have not always been good stewards of Your gift. We have given our time to that which does not satisfy us, does not refresh us, does not make a difference in our lives or in the lives of our brothers and sisters. We have filled our time too full, and have declined your invitation to come and rest. We have been content to fill our lives doing many things, instead of seeking that which we are called to do. Forgive us, O Lord, when we divide our lives into Your time and our time, for You are Lord over all of the hours of all of our days. Forgive us, O Lord.

We pray for those whose days are filled with too many responsibilities, too many tasks. And we pray as well for those whose days are empty, and seem to stretch out forever. For all of them, and for all of us, we pray for your peace, for your rest that brings not only refreshment but renewal.

Teach us, O Lord, to be good stewards of all that we have received. Teach us, O Lord, to recognize in our common days Your uncommon grace.

In the name of Jesus Christ our Lord, who both sought the crowds and withdrew from them, we pray. Amen.

†††

God who has created us
    and who continues to sustain us by Your loving grace,
        we give You thanks for the beauty of Your creation.
We thank You for the variety that is around us—
    the flowers starting to bloom,
    and the trees starting to bud,
    and the gardens now being planted.
For the beauty and wonder and variety of Your earth,
    we give You thanks.
We also give You thanks for the variety of people around us, for in Your loving creation no two of us are just alike in our looks, thought, or speech. We thank You that we are not a "cookie-cutter" creation.

But we confess, O Lord, that sometimes we are frightened by our differences. We confess that we don't know how to act around those who are different in their ability to learn, to hear, to see, or to walk. And so we build walls to separate us from them and to protect ourselves from our own feelings.

Forgive us, O Lord, when in our ignorance, fear, or apathy we forget that all people are made in Your image. Break down the walls that we build among ourselves,
    walls that limit our vision,
    walls that divide Your family.
    In the name of Christ, we pray. Amen.

Almighty God,
   who is our Creator and Redeemer,
   who is both the giver of our peace and the disturber of it, hear
this the prayer of Your children.

We have gathered for worship for many reasons, some
inspiring and noble, some routine, some grudging. Yet for all of us,
there is something deep within us that calls out to be shown the
way. For the journey is difficult, and sometimes we don't know
which way to turn. Which way do we go when the pain within us
will not let us rest? Sometimes, O Lord, we seek not so much a
road to travel but a place where we can stand, where we can
endure.

Which way do we go to find the way of healing for old and
ancient wounds? Which way do we go when life presents us with
too many choices? Which way do we go when life presents us with
no choices and we feel trapped? Where is the way, O Lord, that
will call from us all that is good and strong within us? Where is
the way that will wear away all that is false within us, so that we
might more nearly be the children You created us to be?

Even as we ask, we confess that too often our seeking has been
half-hearted. We have cried out for a word from You, but we have
not listened to the Word that You have spoken to Your people
down through the ages, the Word of God that comes to us as well,
the Word of God that comes for us.

Forgive us, O Lord, and open our eyes. Open our ears. Most of
all, open our hearts to seek You,
   to love You,
   to follow You,
   to walk with You in the way of life.
We pray in the name of Jesus Christ our Lord,
   who is the Way, the Truth, and the Life. Amen.

✝✝✝

Lord our God,
   who has created us and redeemed us,
   who sustains us by your love, mercy, and grace,
      we offer up the prayers of our hearts to You.

We offer up our praise and thanksgiving. We thank You for the gift of creation, and for the gift of one another. But we confess that we have misused both. Forgive us, O Lord, for the casual way that we have treated this good earth. And forgive us for the casual way that we have treated each other. We run from each other's need and are envious of each other's celebrations.

And we confess, O Lord, that oftentimes this gospel of Yours is both confusing and troubling, for it calls into question our most basic assumptions. We cherish power and strength, but You speak of weakness. We want to make it on our own, but You call us to care for and be cared for by one another. We seek security and concrete assurances, and You point to a journey called faith.

But we do know that You will be with us on that journey. And so we seek Your strength, Your care, Your love. Teach us, O Lord, to trust, even when the questions are hard and the answers uncertain. Teach us, O Lord, to love not only those friends whom we cherish but also the strangers among us. Teach us, O Lord, to be good stewards of all the gifts that we have been given.

In the name of our Lord Christ, who came not to be served but to serve, we pray. Amen.

††† 

Great God whose strength has been our comfort,
    whose presence has been our joy,
    whose grace has been our life,
        hear our prayer.

We give You our praise, for You created the earth and all that is in it. You have graced this planet with beauty and variety, from the small wildflower that blooms but for a moment to ancient trees and mountains, from fireflies that punctuate the night to eagles that soar through the skies. We give You thanks, O God, for this good creation.

You have also graced our lives. Your Presence has been with us since before we were born. Even when we thought we could leave You behind, You would not leave us nor give up on us.

When we have fallen, You mercy has helped us to stand again. When we have hurt, Your love has healed. When we have struggled through the dark nights of the soul, You have been the light that would not go away or go out, no matter how deep the shadows.

Even with this, O Lord, even with all of this we confess that sometimes we find ourselves becoming casual and complacent. Our sense of the holy becomes hum-drum. We begin to believe that we have earned all that we have been given. We take Your grace for granted. Forgive us, O Lord, and preserve within us at least a spark of awe, of wonder, of joy that we have received so great a gift.

You have graced our lives through the lives of others—of family, and of friends who become family for us. You have graced our lives with this community of faith. Open our eyes, O Lord, to our brothers and our sisters. Open our ears to hear their cries. Open our hearts to share their joys. Open our hearts to share their need. Open our hands to take their hands. May the love that we receive from You be the love that we share with one another.

There is a world beyond these walls hungry for such a love— those who struggle for bread and for shelter, and those who struggle for hope. There are children wounded by those whom they trust and adults abandoned by those whom they love. And so we pray for courage and for vision so that the love that we receive from You may be the love that we embody in this world, and for the sake of this world. Amen.

✝✝✝

Holy and loving God,
    whose greatness is unsearchable,
    whose love is unquenchable,
        we give You thanks for the gift of this day . . . for the opportunity and freedom of worship, for Your Word proclaimed and lived out through this world, for the gift of life.

But we confess, O Lord, that we don't always know what to do with the gifts that You have given us. Somehow the packages don't look the way that we thought that they would. It is always more than we bargained for; sometimes it is more than we believe that we can bear.

For You give to us a gift of grace, but it's all wrapped up in a call to discipleship. You give us the gift of the light of Your presence, but sometimes it illumines more of our lives than we care to see. You offer to us the gift of being Your sons and daughters when what we'd really like to be are the spectators at Your parade. You give us the gift of life, then call us to die.

Somehow it is always more than we bargained for. Sometimes it is more than we believe that we can bear. And we confess, O God, that sometimes we long for a God whose ways are simple and easily understood, who calls us to certain pathways always filled with light.

But then that would be a god made in our image. And we are the ones who have been made in Your image. So call us forth to be all that we have been created to be. Grant us the courage to accept Your gifts, the strength to follow Your call, the vision to be Your people. In the name of Christ our Lord, Word become flesh, God with us, we pray. Amen.

†††

Holy and loving God,
    who created the universe in all of its vast space, and yet who knows even the hairs of our heads, we offer to You our praise. For You alone are worthy of our praise, our thanksgiving, our allegiance, our all.

Forgive us, Lord, when we do not offer to You all of our strength, preferring to keep some of it for our own pursuits, for fighting our own battles. Too many times we grow impatient with waiting for Your leading and Your direction, and so do things our own way instead.

Forgive us, O Lord, when we do not offer to You all of our weaknesses. Sometimes we would rather cling to them—failures to brood over, hurts to nurse, anger to flame. Forgive us when we would rather hide behind them like a fortress wall than to risk walking with You in the open.

Forgive us, O Lord, when we have not offered to You our hearts, our souls, and our minds. Like a mighty wind that disturbs the landscape, may Your Spirit come among us. Like a gentle breeze that gently caresses the leaves, may Your Spirit come among us.

Be Thou our vision, O Lord, to lead us on from here. Capture us in Your grace. Warm us with Your love. Kindle within us a flame that will not die, come what may. In the name of Christ our Lord, we pray. Amen.

†††

Lord of all grace and God of all glory, We praise You, for You alone are God. We praise You for the wonder and expanse of Your creation. For the delightful, delight-filled variety of Your creatures, including humankind, we give You thanks and praise. We give You thanks, O God. For You called us out, even when we did not know Your name. You saved us, even when we did not, do not deserve such a gift. You continue to be with us, loving us, sustaining us, responding to us with grace. Time and again we stumble and fall in our haste to get away from You. But still You are there, helping us up, brushing us off, healing our bumps and bruises and scrapes and scratches. Perhaps even gently laughing with us when we discover how foolish we looked in the midst of it all.

And yet, we confess that sometimes we make it all too neat and easy and orderly for ourselves. We no longer stumble, for we are neither bold enough to run away from You nor courageous enough to run to you. Forgive us when You simply become a part of our routine—safe, comfortable, predictable. Forgive us, O Lord, when we would rather read the guidebooks and watch the travelogue than risk traveling this journey of faith ourselves. Forgive us, O Lord.

Hear, O God, the cries of our hearts. Hear the cries of this Your creation—the cries for freedom . . . the cries for hope . . . the cries of the hungry and the thirsty who long to be filled. Hear our cries, O Lord. Heal us and help us on the way to being Your people, that we, too, might hear the cries of creation; that we might also bring healing and hope to this world. Amen.

†††

God of hope and God of life,

You who knows us intimately, who loves us unconditionally, who cares for us beyond all measure or deserving, we open our hearts to You.

We open to You the bright, glad places of celebration, where our hope shines and joy dances within us. For all that makes our spirits soar and our hearts sing, we give You thanks.

We open to You the frightened and uncertain places, the places within us that ring with questions, that are hammered by doubts. Places of fear of what might be. Places torn by difficult decisions. In our best moments, we know that it is not so much the answers to our questions that we seek but Your presence in the midst of them.

And slowly, even reluctantly, we open to you the dark places. We confess, O Lord, that there are deep shadows within us. shadows of selfishness and greed. Shadows that gleefully seek revenge, shadows that lash out to hurt even those whom we would love the most. Shadows that call us not to care about the pain and hunger of the rest of the world as long as we are safe, full, and successful. Forgive us, O Lord. And teach us how to pray for one another, how to love one another.

Help us to seek You with all of our hearts,
to love You with all of our minds,
to follow You not just for one hour a week,
but for all of the hours of all of our days. Amen.

Lord God, our Creator, Redeemer and Sustainer,

The heavens tell of Your glory and the earth sings Your praises, from the gentle splash of the azalea to the songs of the birds that embroider the early morning air. All of this points to a God who, out of extravagant love, gives not only what is necessary and useful, but also what is enjoyable and beautiful. We give You thanks. And if we would but listen to the rhythm of our lives, we would find the music of praise springing forth there as well. For You, O Lord, have been with us. Before we were yet born, You cared for us. In the shadow places of our lives, You have been light that will not fail. When it seemed that we could not go on, You have been our strength for one more step.

In the face of all that has gone before, O Lord, it seems that it should be easy to believe. But we confess that even now our faith is sometimes a crazy quilt stitched together with mostly fear and doubt. We find it hard to believe. Sometimes the darkness within us seems so deep that we wonder if even Your light can penetrate it. We are afraid of what You will ask us to give, and to give up. We are afraid of who You will call us to be. We suspect that if we walk with You that sooner or later we will wind up at a cross.

And yet, deep within us, we know that only in You are we made whole. Only by following You can we fully be ourselves. And if Your way leads to a cross, it also leads to life. In Your grace is our strength. In Your love is our joy. In Your presence is our peace, now and forevermore. Amen.

†††

Eternal God, who has created us, who has loved us, who has cared for us as a parent cares for a child,

We give You thanks for the children in our midst. For the babies, fresh with the hope of new life; for children who are growing, learning—and sometimes teaching us. For the blessed uniqueness, for the holy promise of children, we give You thanks.

But we confess, O Lord, that sometimes we view childhood through rose-colored glasses. We see only the fun, and not the fear. We hear only the laughter, and not the cries. Forgive us, O Lord, when we turn away, for it makes us uncomfortable to believe that for some, childhood is a painful, rocky road. . . .

The AIDS babies, who are born under the shadow of death before they ever have a chance at life;

Children, even in this prosperous country, whose minds, bodies, and futures are stunted by the lack of food;

Children whose playmates are violence and poverty;

Children whose homes and families are not safe havens but rather places of fear and of danger, of abuse and neglect.

Forgive us, O Lord, when we do not see, when we do not speak, when we do not care for all of our children. For they are Your children as well.

May we speak for those who have no voice. May we stand for those who have no vote. May we make a welcome place for all of the children of this world.

In the name of Christ our Lord, we pray. Amen.

†††

## Prayers for Special Services

*(For Pentecost Sunday)*

God of our past,
    who has sustained us from one generation to the next;
God of our future,
    who holds our days to come in the safety of Your hand;
God of this present hour,
    we give You thanks.

We give You thanks for all of the times that by the power of Your Holy Spirit, you have guided us, sustained us, strengthened us. Sometimes we knew the time of Your coming. We felt the power and grace of Your Spirit in a moment of worship, a word of encouragement, a glimpse of beauty that moved us and gave us hope. And sometime we didn't know what happened or why, but when we had no strength to go on, we found the courage to take one more step. Only in remembering did we realize that You were with us. For such times, we give You thanks.

Forgive us, O Lord, when we take the gift of Your Spirit too lightly, when it becomes a good-luck charm or a refuge of last resort. Forgive us when we speak too glibly of such mystery. For Your Spirit is a fire that we cannot control and a wind that we cannot command. And we confess that sometimes we are afraid to open our lives to such a Spirit. For if such a force takes hold of us, we shall surely be changed.

And yet, there are hurts deep within us that cry out for healing. There is grief heavy upon us that cries out for comfort. There is longing deep within us to do more . . . and to be more, but alone we have neither the strength nor the vision.

We do not know where Your Spirit will lead us, O Lord. But we know, somewhere in the deep places of our hearts, that we cannot live without it. So come, Holy Spirit, and make Your home among us. Amen.

†††

*(For a Service Celebrating Baptism)*

Giver of life, whose grace is sufficient and whose love is abundant, O Lord our God, hear our prayers.

Hear our thanks, for we confess that we do not give You thanks often enough. We take Your gifts for granted, as we have earned the right to have them. In our best moments, we know that's not so. So for the gift of life, and for Your presence in our lives that brings to us meaning and purpose, strength and comfort, we give You thanks. For the gift of those with whom we share our lives, we give You thanks. And for the gift of the great communion of saints whose light still shines, whose faith still endures, we give You thanks.

Hear this our prayer, O Lord, for this Your daughter who has chosen to follow You in baptism this day. Your grace has brought her along in the way of faith, now You lead her in new pathways. We ask that Your Spirit continue to be with her that she might grow in faith, hope, and love.

Hear this our confession, O Lord. For we confess that sometimes we forget that we are not our own. We live our lives as if we were the sole captains of our fate. We make our decisions, we go about our days as if our faith were nothing but a footnote. We confess that at times we have chosen to be molded and formed in the image of this world.

We gather before the baptismal waters on this day. On this day, whether for the first time or the thousandth time, may we hear the calling of our Lord to follow. We gather around the table this day. On this day, whether for the first time or the thousandth time, may we share this meal as those who have chosen to bear the name of Christ and to walk in his way.

In losing our lives for Your sake, may we find joy that knows no measure and the peace that goes beyond all understanding. For we pray in the name of our Lord Christ, Amen.

†††

*(For a Service Celebrating Baptism)*

God of all life, who gifts us with life and graces us with faith,
we come to celebrate and to give thanks for these Your children,
and for the journey that they have begun. We give You thanks for
all who have touched their lives in Your name—parents and
family, teachers and friends. May their years ahead be filled with
those who will encourage them, who will teach by word and by
example, who will help them ask questions and to struggle for the
answers. May their lives be filled with many who by their love
and their lives will point the way to You.

We confess, O God, that there is much in our lives that has
been birthed and yet has not grown. Too soon we forget that You
not only call us away from old life, you call us forward to new life.
Too many faith journeys have been begun, only to never be trav-
elled. Detours and doubts sidetrack us.

Forgive us, O Lord, and make of us new creations. We know
not what Your grace will demand of us, but grant to us the
strength to respond. We know not where this journey will lead us,
but grant to us patience when the way leads through wilderness
and joy when our way leads beside still waters. We know not
what new thing may yet be born within us. May we encourage
and guide one another. May we be led by Your Spirit.

For we know that our lives are incomplete without Your
presence, our promise is unfulfilled apart from You. So we offer to
You our lives and our prayers, in the name of Christ our Lord.
Amen.


†††


*(Prayer of Dedication for Workers)*

Great God, giver of all good gifts,
    We thank you for the gifts represented here,
        and for these your children
            who are willing to share of themselves.

We ask for your blessing upon them,
  and Your presence with them,
        to give them strength when the way is difficult,
        to give them patience when the road is long,
        to share in their joy when dreams come to life,
        to grant them grace when dreams stumble.
For this your church, we pray.
    May our hands be strong enough to do the work before us.
    May our hearts be tender enough to respond with love.
Help us, O Lord,
    to see one another's gifts,
    and to encourage one another in service.
        Bless these your servants, O Lord,
            that we might be faithful.
In the name of Jesus Christ our Lord,
    who came among us as one who serves,
        we pray. Amen.


✝✝✝


*(Prayer of Dedication for Workers)*

Bless these Your servants, O Lord.
Grant to them hearts made tender by Your love and compassion.
Grant to them arms made strong by the power of Your presence.
Grant to them minds eager to know more of You and Your Word.
Grant to them a will colored and shaped by your will.
    Bless these Your servants, O Lord.
Bless the gifts that they offer to this Your church.
May they build up the body of Christ.
May they bring hope and healing and love.
May they be used always for Your glory.
    And for this church, we pray.
May we be wise stewards of the gifts among us,
    that none go neglected, unused, or wasted.

Grant to us the grace to see in one another our calling to be
servants,
     grant to us the grace to live out that calling.
In the name of Jesus Christ our Lord, we pray, Amen.


†††


*(For a Service of Recognition/Dedication of Parents/Children)*

Great and loving God,
     giver of all life,
          we are gathered this morning with our thoughts turned
towards family . . .
     the folks who gave life to us, who nurtured us.
     For mothers who carried us and cared for us,
     we give You thanks.
     But even filled with the warm glow of this service, we know
that for some this day brings more pain than celebration. For those
who mourn the loss of mother or father, for those whose parents
are aging and face uncertain days filled with difficult decisions, we
pray. There are those who feel torn between the needs of parents
and the needs of children, and for them we pray.
     For some this day is an empty reminder of children that once
were or may never be. And then there are the children—
     children who struggle for life,
     children who suffer neglect,
     children with no parents, no family.
We confess that sometimes we would like to ignore those who do
not fit into our Norman Rockwell Mother's Day pictures. We
would rather be blind to them than be bothered by them.
     And so we come to You, O God, asking You to rejoice with
those who rejoice this day, and weep with those who weep. Hear
the prayers of our hearts rising up this day. For we pray in the
name of our Lord Christ. Amen.

†††

*(Prayer of Dedication for Children)*

Great and gracious God, who has given us life and who has given
our lives meaning by Your presence,
    we celebrate these young lives that You have given to us, and
we ask Your blessing upon them.
    Lay upon them Your hands of love,
        that they will always know how very precious
            they are to You—and to us.
    Lay upon them Your hands of grace,
        so that when they fall or falter,
        they will know that You are there to help them up again.
    Lay upon them Your hands of hope,
    that they will grow up to dream bold dreams,
        and lay upon them Your hands of courage
            so that they might bring those dreams to life.
    Lay upon them Your hands of light,
        so that Your light might shine through them.
    Lay upon them Your hands of joy,
        so that their lives might be filled with laughter.
Bless these children, O God, for we dedicate them to You.
And in so doing, we renew our own dedication to You so that our
lives might be a word of blessing upon the lives of our children.
As family and friends, as their family of faith, help us to be good
stewards of the lives with which we have been entrusted. In the
name of Jesus Christ, who welcomed the children, we pray. Amen.

✝✝✝

# The Christian Year

## Advent

### Calls to Worship

Leader: Our Lord, we enter this season of Advent, and our hearts echo the church's plea. Come, Lord Jesus.

**People: Come into these days too filled and hours too hurried and be our peace. Come, Lord Jesus.**

Leader: Come into this troubled and hurting world and be our hope. Come, Lord Jesus.

**People: Come into this season of light and be our soul's true light. Come, Lord Jesus.**

Leader: Come into this time of celebration and be our joy. Come, Lord Jesus.

**People: Come into our lives and be life for us, now and forevermore.**

Leader: Come and be Emmanuel—God with us.

**People: God for us.**

**All: Amen.**

### †††

Leader: There is a song that fills the air in these days.

**People: More than canned carols, it is a song of hope for those who despair.**

Leader: A song of love for those who have been wounded.

**People: A song of peace for those whose hearts are restless.**

Leader: A song of celebration for those whose joy is full.

**People: A song for children.**

Leader: A song for adults.

**People: A song fills the air these days.**

Leader: May this melody of God's grace also fill our hearts and spill out into our lives.

**People: May this Advent season be filled with the music of God's love.**

## Invocations

God of light,
  God of peace,
we gather together to celebrate a story that is old and familiar,
yet something within us cries out to hear it anew. In the well-worn
words, may we be surprised again by the mystery and wonder of
your grace. In the familiar notes, may we hear creation's song of
celebration that rings through the ages. Be Thou with us as we
hear and celebrate this ancient story
    that we might hear our story,
    that we might find our life. Amen.


†††


In a world that has grown cynical with waiting, O Lord,
    in a world that does not believe
        what it cannot see and touch right now,
            we have lit a candle called promise.
In a world full of the darkness of fear
    and prejudice and misunderstanding,
    we have lit a candle called light.
In a world that finds bigger and better ways to hate each other,
    we have lit a candle called love.
Sometimes it all seems so foolish.
But by Your Presence,
    turn our foolishness into wisdom. Amen.


†††


May our sophistication never become so great
    that we forget the wonder of Your gift.
May our celebration never become so elaborate
    that we forget the simplicity of Your Son's birth.
May we never suppose our knowledge to be so great
    that we forget the mystery of Your love. Amen.

God who is the maker of all things
   and the giver of all gifts,
We come this morning to celebrate.
We come to celebrate a birth that brings life—
   not just to one infant,
   but to all of us,
      for all of us.
We come to celebrate the birth
   not only of a baby,
      but of hope,
      of love made flesh,
      of God with us.
Come, Emmanuel,
   and be with us now as we worship You this day. Amen.

✝✝✝

## Litanies

Leader:    In the midst of the busyness of these days, we seek a time and a place and a reason to stop.

**People:    In the midst of plastic carols, we seek a song that is genuine and real.**

Leader:    In the midst of so many Christmas stories, we seek a story that is worth remembering and re-telling.

**People:    In the midst of so many lights and so much glitter, we seek a light that is lasting and eternal.**

Leader:    In this hour of worship, may we who seek, find.

**People:    May we who seek, be found.**

✝✝✝

Leader:  Before mystery,
**People:  We stand in wonder.**
Leader:  Before miracle,
**People:  We stand in awe.**
Leader:  Before love incarnate,
**People:  We stand amazed.**
Leader:  God be with us in our worship, lest our words be too
         eager and glib.
**People:  God be with us to surprise us once again with Your
         grace.**

†††

## Prayers

O Lord our God,
   Be Thou with us as we worship You,
That in the midst of the noise of our lives
   we might yet hear the songs of angels.
In the midst of Christmas lights
   we may yet meet the light of the world.
In the midst of the ups and downs of these days,
   we may walk with the One who has come
         to bear our grief and complete our joy.
Come and be with us that our holidays may yet be holy days.
Amen.

†††

O God who became flesh and dwelt among us,
   we give You thanks for this season of Advent.
   We give You thanks for familiar music and comforting traditions. We give You thanks for the grace of family and friends, for
gifts given. Not only the tangible kind wrapped in paper and
bows, but other gifts as well—a hug, a handshake, laughter shared,

love expressed. Most of all, we give You thanks for the gift of Your son that brings us light, that gives us hope, that makes our celebration something more than whistling in the dark.

But there are others for whom these are difficult days. There are those for whom holiday traditions mean fresh reminders of grief not yet healed. Others stand by helplessly while loved ones linger in the chasm between life and death. For these we pray, asking for them Your peace that goes beyond all understanding, for Your love that goes beyond all fear.

And for ourselves, we pray. Forgive us, O Lord, if we have let all of the trappings of this season crowd out the meaning of it. Forgive us if the nativity scene has become obscured by wrapping paper and tinsel and colored lights. And forgive us, O Lord, if we dare to walk away from Christmas untouched and unchanged, if having heard it all before, we miss seeing the Christ who still comes to us. Grant to us ears to hear, eyes to see, and a story to tell of a God who still becomes flesh and walks among us.
Amen.

††† 

Almighty God,
In a world heavy with the threat of war,
    we come to celebrate the Prince of Peace.
In a time characterized by greed and selfishness,
    we come to rejoice in Your selfless gift.
In an age burdened by despair and lack of hope,
    we come to announce the advent of the Promised One.
In a society self-defined by success,
    we come to encounter the Suffering Servant.
In the midst of a people who have lost their direction,
    we come seeking the One who is the Way,
            the Truth,
            the Life.

O Lord our God,

we come to celebrate the birth of Your Son, to proclaim light in a world of darkness. As we join together in this simple service, may we be a community not simply in word but also in spirit.

As we anticipate Christmas, may we seek the path that leads us inward to You while leading us outward to our brothers and our sisters in the world.

In the name of the newborn baby in the stable
and the young man on the cross, we pray.
Amen.

†††

## Affirmations of Faith

## The First Sunday in Advent

We believe in God who has been made known to us through Jesus Christ, the Son of God. He became flesh and went about doing God's work in this world. But many who saw him did not recognize him and did not welcome him. They crucified him, but on the third day God raised him from the dead.

We believe that this Jesus of Nazareth, who is also the Christ, will come again to this creation, bringing with him the fullness of God's kingdom. He comes, not at our whim nor by our schedules, but according to the mystery of the will of God.

We believe that we who are called by the name of Christ as Christians are also called to be about the work of Christ until he comes. By the power of God's Holy Spirit, we proclaim and live out the love and grace of God. By the power of God's Holy Spirit, we live as the people of God's kingdom, until the day that God's kingdom comes on earth. Amen.

†††

## The Second Sunday in Advent

We believe in God, who created us and loves us. We believe in Jesus Christ, the Son of God, the One to whom John bore witness. We believe that Jesus came preaching a word of repentance, and that we, like his first hearers, are also called to turn away from our sin, to become new creations born not of water but by the grace of God. We are called out of our darkness into God's marvelous light.

We believe in the sustaining presence of God's Holy Spirit, in whose power we find the strength to confess our sin, the healing touch of God's mercy and forgiveness, and the love of God that offers to us life everlasting. Amen.

†††

## The Third Sunday In Advent

We believe in God, the creator of the universe, and in Jesus Christ, God's Son. We believe that his ministry on earth was marked by compassion for the hurting, welcome for the outcast, hope for the abandoned, and healing for the sick. He confronted those for whom religion replaced holiness and for whom self-righteousness replaced right living.

We believe that Jesus was fully human and fully divine, and that he calls us, his sisters and brothers, to join with him in his ministry of justice and mercy.

We believe in the empowering presence of God's Holy Spirit to give us clear eyes with which to see injustice, tender hearts to share in this world's suffering, and open hands to give of ourselves. Amen.

†††

## Fourth Sunday In Advent

We believe in God, maker of all things, and in Jesus Christ, God's Son and our Lord. We believe that Jesus became as we are, being born into this world as a helpless infant, facing the challenges of childhood and the temptations of adulthood. We believe that he has shared both our joys and our sorrows.

We believe that in Jesus, God spoke to this world in a new way. In Jesus, the Word became flesh and dwelt among us, embodying God's steadfast love and mercy.

We believe that through God's Holy Spirit, God continues to speak to our world. We believe that the same grace that Jesus taught and lived out throughout his ministry is available to us today. Amen.

✝✝✝

## Lighting of the Advent Candles

*(These may be modified by having a person read the initial scripture passage, to be followed by response as indicated.)*

## The Candle of Hope

Leader:     Hear the words of our God:
            "I know the plans I have for you, says the Lord, plans for welfare and not for evil, to give you a future and a hope."

**People:    "Then you will call upon me and come and pray to me, and I will hear you."**

Leader:     "You will seek me and find me; when you seek me with all your heart." (Jer 29:11-13)

**People:    Our world is all too familiar with the dark words of despair.**

Leader:     But we are not alone, for God has remembered us.

**People:    This day we light the candle of hope.**

Leader:     We are not alone, for God has cared for us.

**People:    May the light of hope burn brightly in our lives and in our world.**

## The Candle of Promise

Leader:    Hear the words of the prophet:
        "God will swallow up death for ever."

**People:**    **"And the Lord God will wipe away tears from all faces and the reproach of his people God will take away from the earth, for he has spoken."**

Leader:    "It will be said on that day,"

**People:**    **"Lo, this is our God, we have waited that he might save us. This is the Lord; we have waited for him";**

Leader:    "Let us be glad and rejoice in his salvation."
        (Isa 25:8–9)

**People:**    **Our world knows much of promises casually made and easily broken.**

Leader:    But we may trust the promises of this God,
        for God's faithfulness has been proven throughout all generations.

**People:**    **This day we light the candle of promise.**

Leader:    We wait with joy for the coming of our Lord.

**People:**    **May the promise of God sparkle in our lives and in our world.**

†††

## The Candle of Light

Leader:    Hear the words of the prophet:
        "The people who walked in darkness have seen a great light";

**People:**    **"Those who lived in a land of deep darkness—on them the light has shined. . . ."**

Leader:    "For a child has been born for us, a son given to us";

**People:**    **"Authority rests upon his shoulders, and he shall be called Wonderful Counselor, Mighty God, Everlasting Father, Prince of Peace." (Isa 9:2,6)**

**People:**      **Our world knows much of the darkness of fear and hatred.**

Leader:      But we have seen God's light of peace and love.

**People:**      **This day we light the candle of light.**

Leader:      May the light of God's presence illumine our lives and our world.


†††


## The Candle of Joy

Leader:      Hear the words of the prophet:
             "Surely God is my salvation";

**People:**      **"I will trust and not be afraid, for the Lord God is my strength and my might; he has become my salvation."**

Leader      "With joy you will draw water from the wells of salvation."

**People:**      **"And you will say in that day, 'Give thanks to the Lord, call on his name; make known his deeds among the nations, proclaim that his house is exalted.' . . ."**

Leader:      "Shout aloud and sing for joy, O royal Zion, for great in your midst is the Holy One of Israel." (Isa 12:2–6)

**People:**      **Our world knows much of sorrow and sadness.**

Leader:      But we may rejoice, for our God has come to turn our weeping into laughter, our mourning into gladness.

**People:**      **This day we light the candle of joy.**

Leader:      May the brightness of God's gift of joy shine in our world and in our lives.

*(The following four Advent candles are based on the text from Isaiah 61:1–3, the same passage that Jesus read in the synagogue in Nazareth at the beginning of his ministry [Luke 4:16–20]. Using these texts helps the congregation to focus not only on the coming of Christ, but the character of his mission and ministry.)*

## The Candle of Good News

*(Isa 61:1-2a is read.)*

Leader: Today we light the Candle of Good News. Let this light shine.

**People: Wherever songs are silenced and voices stilled by fear and oppression, let this light shine.**

Leader: Wherever truth is locked away, let this light shine.

**People: Wherever there are people who are oppressed by the chains of prejudice, the shackles of hatred and the stealing away of hope, let this light shine.**
*(The candle is lit.)*

Leader: And Jesus said, "The Lord has sent me to bring good news to the oppressed."

**People: May this light shine.**

✝✝✝

## The Candle of Healing

*(Isa 61:1-2a is read.)*

Leader: Today we light the Candle of Healing. Let this light shine.

**People: Wherever trust has been betrayed and dreams have been shattered, let this light shine.**

Leader: Wherever grief has made its home, let this light shine.

**People: Wherever there are people who are wounded and weary, anxious and hurting, let this light shine.**
*(The candle is lit.)*

Leader:    And Jesus said, "The Lord has anointed me . . . to bind
           up the brokenhearted."
**People:    Let this light shine.**

✝✝✝

## The Candle of Freedom

*(Isa 61:1-2a is read.)*
Leader:    Today we light the Candle of Freedom.
**People:    Wherever conscience is held captive and liberty denied,
           let this light shine.**
Leader:    Wherever people are imprisoned by their enemies, let
           this light shine.
**People:    Wherever prisons are self-made and condemning hearts
           are jailers, let this light shine.**
           *(The candle is lit.)*
Leader:    And Jesus said, "The Lord has sent me . . . to proclaim
           liberty to the captives and release to the prisoners."
**People:    Let this light shine.**

✝✝✝

## The Candle of Grace

*(Isa 62:1-2a is read.)*
Leader:    Today we light the Candle of Grace.
**People:    Wherever people have fallen short or fallen by the
           wayside, let this light shine.**
Leader:    Wherever there are people longing to be accepted and
           hearts longing to be heard, let this light shine.
**People:    Wherever pilgrims are searching for a home, let this
           light shine.**
           *(The candle is lit.)*
Leader:    And Jesus said, "The Spirit of the Lord is upon me,
           because he has anointed me . . . to proclaim the year of
           the Lord's favor."
**People:    Let this light shine.**

## The Lighting of The Christ Candle

Leader:    Into the waiting night, the Christ child is born.

**People:    Into the silent night, songs of joy and wonder ring forth.**

Leader:    Into the darkness of the world's night, the light of the world has come.

**People:    Christ, our Lord, is born!**

Leader:    The light of his candle burns before us.

**People:    The light of his love burns within us.**

Leader:    Christ, our Lord, is born.

All:    Let us rejoice and give thanks.

†††

# Lent

Leader: For God so loved the world that he gave his only Son, that whoever believes in him should not perish but have eternal life.

People: **In this is love, not that we loved God, but that God loved us and sent God's Son.**

Leader: Have this mind among yourselves which is yours in Christ Jesus, who though he was in the form of God did not count equality with God a thing to be grasped, but emptied himself, taking the form of a servant, being born in human likeness.

People: **And being found in human form he humbled himself and became obedient unto death, even death on a cross.**

Leader: And Jesus said, "Love one another as I have loved you. Greater love has no one than this, that a person lay down his life for his friends."

Choir: *(singing)*
*Were the whole realm of nature mine*
*That were a present far too small;*
*Love so amazing, so divine*
*Demands my soul, my life, my all.*
(From "When I Survey the Wondrous Cross" by Isaac Watts)

†††

Leader: In this is love, not that we loved God but that God loved us and sent God's Son.

People: **We come to worship the One who knows our pain, for he himself suffered.**

Leader: We come to worship to One who knows our tears, for he himself has wept.

People: **We come to worship the One who knows our loneliness, for he himself was abandoned.**

Leader: We come to worship the One who knows our dying, for he himself was killed.

People:   **This Jesus we seek to follow, for in Him is our life and our hope.**

Leader:   Let us worship God together.

✝✝✝

Leader:   "Jesus set his face toward Jerusalem." (Luke 9:51)

People:   **Our Lord is on a journey, and the way leads through opposition and misunderstanding.**

Leader:   Jesus invites us to follow him.

People:   **This journey leads through the shadows of betrayal, the night of Gethsemane, the afternoon darkness of Golgotha.**

Leader:   "Then Jesus told his disciples, 'If any want to become my followers, let them deny themselves and take up their cross and follow me. For those who want to save their life will lose it, and those who lose their life for my sake will find it.' " (Matt 16:24-25)

People:   **Our Lord is on a journey. May we have the grace to follow this Christ, and to give to him our very lives. For in giving away our lives, we find them, and in dying we live.**

✝✝✝

Leader:   The church embraces the season of Lent, a time for reflection.

People:   **We are busy people with places to go and things to do. We haven't the time to stop.**

Leader:   The church embraces the season of Lent, a time for prayer.

People:   **Our lives are filled with noise and confusion. We haven't the space for the silence of prayer.**

Leader:     The church embraces the season of Lent, a time for con-
            fession and repentance.

**People:    Too much talk of sin makes us uncomfortable. We'd
            rather not examine our choices too closely or take
            responsibility for our actions.**

Leader:     The church gathers for the season of Lent. And in our
            gathering we are met by the grace of God that forgives
            our sin, transforms our lives, and gives to us the prom-
            ise of a life without end.

**Choir:     "So Jesus asked the twelve, 'Do you also wish to go
            away?' Simon Peter answered him, 'Lord, to whom can
            we go? You have the words of eternal life.' " (John
            6:67–68)**

Leader:     The church gathers for the season of Lent, and all are
            welcome.

# Holy Week

## Maundy Thursday

Leader: And Jesus said, "The greatest love a person can have for his friends is to lay down his life for them."

People: **We gather to recall the night in which Jesus was betrayed.**

Leader: "You are my friends if you do what I command you. This I command you, to love one another."

People: **We gather to share a common table as sisters and brothers.**

Leader; "My peace I give to you. Be of good cheer, for I have overcome the world."

People: **Even in this hour of darkness, we gather to praise the God of our salvation.**

✝✝✝

## Easter

Leader: He is alive!

People: **The stone across the entrance of the grave could not keep him locked away. He is alive!**

Leader: Soldiers and guards could not keep him locked away. He is alive!

People: **All of the cruelty and hate of this world could not keep him locked away. He is alive!**

Leader: Death itself could not keep him. He is alive! Let us rejoice.

All: *(singing)*
*Rejoice, the Lord is King;*
*Your Lord and King adore!*

*Rejoice, give thanks and sing
And triumph evermore.
Lift up your heart, lift up Your voice!
Rejoice, Again I say rejoice!*

††† 

Leader:    We come to speak, for there is good news that must be spoken.
People:    **We come to sing, for all of creation is bursting with great, glad alleluias.**
All:    *We come to worship, for in the quiet places of our hearts we hope that we, too, will hear the sound of our name, that we will meet our Lord, by love's power risen, bringing to us hope and light and life.*
(From "Rejoice, the Lord is King" by Charles Wesley)

††† 

Leader:    Sing alleluia, for Christ our Lord is risen.
People:    **"Do not be afraid," said the angel to the women at the tomb.**
Leader:    Sing alleluia, for death has been defeated.
People:    **"Do not be afraid," said Jesus to his disciples.**
Leader:    Sing alleluia, for God's love has triumphed over evil.
People:    **We sing with joy, for there is nothing that can ever separate us from the love of God.**
Leader:    If God be for us, then who can be against us?
People:    **With a word of comfort, a word of hope,**
Leader:    With a word of love
All:    *Christ is risen!*
People:    **Let us rejoice and give thanks.**

†††

| | |
|---|---|
| Leader: | The Lord is risen! |
| **People:** | **The Lord is risen indeed.** |
| Leader: | Death has finally been defeated, for Christ our Lord is risen. |
| **People:** | **Hope has been vindicated, for Christ our Lord is risen.** |
| Leader: | Love has triumphed, for Christ our Lord is risen. |
| **People:** | **Let us rejoice, for Christ our Lord is risen.** |
| *All:* | *Alleluia!* |

†††

| | |
|---|---|
| Leader: | Hear the glad news—Jesus Christ is risen! |
| **People:** | **He faced the agony of the cross.** |
| Leader: | He is alive! |
| **People:** | **He faced the silence of the tomb.** |
| Leader: | He is risen! |
| **People:** | **Jesus Christ is risen, and in his life we find our life.** |
| Leader: | Let us rejoice, and give thanks. |

†††

| | |
|---|---|
| Leader: | It is Easter Sunday, and the world is turned upside down. |
| **People:** | **In the emptiness of the tomb, we find the fullness of hope.** |
| Leader: | The end is the beginning. |
| **People:** | **And death becomes life.** |
| Leader: | It is Easter Sunday morning, and the world is turned upside down. |
| **People:** | **Let us rejoice, for in the topsy-turvy world of God's kingdom, we find our true life.** |

†††

# Hymn Texts

## Come Our Sisters, Come Our Brothers

Come our sisters, come our brothers
Claim with joy your rightful place.
Every pattern, every color
Joined in the bright quilt of faith.
Come and sing your songs of wisdom,
Come and share your vision true.
All are welcome in God's kingdom
Where our Lord makes all things new.

Find your place in quiet hearing,
Join with Mary, free to learn.
Find your place in dawn's bright garden
With the women, last to mourn.
Find your place, with them commissioned
To be preachers of the Word,
Of the love that lives unconquered,
Of the good news of our Lord.

Come our sisters, come our brothers,
Claim with joy your rightful place.
Not by ruling but by serving,
Not by power but by grace.
Come with hope and come with courage;
God is calling, leading still.
Let us then join hands and voices
God's high calling to fulfill.

(Tune: ODE TO JOY)

✝✝✝

### Let the Children Come

Let the children come, be welcome
With their laughter and their tears.
Let them come, all shapes and sizes
To Christ's body, gathered here.
Let them come that we might teach them
All the kindness of God's grace;
Let them come that we might show them
Through our lives, a living faith.

Let the children come, be welcome
With their promise and their light.
Let them come, all shapes and sizes,
In their eyes, hope shining bright.
Let them come and be our teachers,
Lessons full of fun and play;
Let them come and be our vision,
Finding wonder each new day.

Let the children come, be welcome,
Children found in ev'ry place.
Let them come, all shapes and sizes,
Let us honor every race.
Let them come, the poor, the hungry,
Let them come, left all alone;
Let them come, who hurt and struggle,
In Christ's body, find a home.

Let the children come, be welcome
Said the Christ, arms opened wide.
And they came, all shapes and sizes
To find welcome by his side.
Children teach us of God's kingdom
By their trust and by their love.
Young and old, we all are children
Of the God who reigns above.

                              (Tune: HOLY MANNA)

## Jesus, Driven by the Spirit

Jesus driven by the Spirit
To the wilderness to pray;
Facing there alone his future,
Fasting there for forty days.
In his hunger he was tempted,
Turning desert stones to bread;
Winning crowds by show of power;
"Have the world," the Tempter said.

Jesus, facing crucial choices
Turned the Tempter's world away;
Choosing to be suff'ring servant
That through him we would be saved.
Not for him a throne of power,
But for him a crown of thorns.
Facing all alone death's darkness,
By his cross, new life is born.

We are led now by God's Spirit
To the wilderness to pray;
Resting hurried hearts in silence
For our Lenten forty days.
Still our lives are full of choices
Of the pathways we would take—
Living only for our glory,
Living only for Christ's sake.

Let us see our faith more clearly
In this lenten, desert air.
Let us see our sin, confessing,
Also find forgiveness there.
Let us hear anew God's calling
To be servants of our Lord;
Through our hymns and prayers reshape us
To be people of Your word.

(Tune: BEECHER)

### Blessed are the Peacemakers

How blest are those who work for peace
Through paths of righteousness,
For they are children of our God;
In God they shall be blessed.

Teach us, O Lord, Your way of love,
The way that leads to peace:
The hungry filled, the hurting healed,
And all the captives freed.

Into the night of greed and strife
We dare to bring God's light,
Against the power of the wrong
We bring the strength of right.

Until all shall know the gift of hope,
And all injustice cease;
Until the day of hate is done,
Lord, let us strive for peace.

††† 

### Come, All Christians, Come
*(Ordination Hymn For Monica Citty Hix)*

Praise be to God, the Spirit and the Son,
Creating God, in whom we are made one;
Join songs of praises, Come, all Christians, come.
Alleluia, Alleluia.

Within the church, we find a welcome place
Where love encircles, nurtures into faith,
And with the saints we learn the songs of grace.
Alleluia, Alleluia.

God's daughters, sons, together are set free
To be Christ's body in a world of need;
Faithful in service may we ever be.
Alleluia, Alleluia.

And now we pray for those whom God calls out,
The Spirit guiding in this present hour;
Love be their strength and weakness be their pow'r.
Alleluia, Alleluia.

(Tune: SINE NOMINE)


†††


## Lord God, We Are Set Free

For freedom, Christ has set us free
By God's great gift of grace;
Forgiven and redeemed are we;
Set free to live by faith.

From fear that turns the day to night,
Old hurts, old wrongs, old grief;
From hidden pain locked deep inside,
Lord God, we are set free.

From heavy burdens of the Law,
Commands we failed to keep;
From failure met along the way,
Lord God, we are set free.

From ceaseless striving to do right,
To prove our worth by deeds;
From all that would enslave our lives,
Lord God, we are set free.

For freedom, Christ has set us free
By God's great gift of grace;
Forgiven and redeemed are we,
Set free to live by faith.

(Tune: ST. ANNE)

✝✝✝

## The Journey of Faith
*(For College Park Baptist Church, Greensboro, NC)*

To a journey God has called us,
To a life of love and hope;
In the light and in the shadow,
God is with us as we go.
Faith that grows with each new challenge,
Trust that leads through paths unknown,
We, as pilgrims, walk together
In the journey to our home.

For the strength of faithful witness
Lived through days of joy and tears;
And the gift of grace sufficient
For the ever-flowing years;
For the richness of Your mercy
To Thee, Lord, we give You our praise.
May our lives reflect Your glory
'Till the close of all our days.

Go we now to be God's people,
Go we now our faith to live.
Help us learn from one another
Faith to keep, a faith to give.
Go we now on life's great journey,
Go we now, but not alone.
With God's people, by God's Spirit,
Faith leads forward, faith leads on.

(Tune: HYFRYDOL)

### Come, Jesus Christ

In the dark calm of Bethl'hem's night,
Within the walls of stable poor,
Comes to the world the gift of light;
Into the world the Christ is born.

Comes to a world where power rules,
Comes to a world where sin holds fast;
Comes in his wisdom as a fool,
Comes as a servant, as the last.

God's love enfleshed, God's grace is he;
He suffers gladly for our sakes.
By Jesus' death he sets us free;
By Jesus' life death's pow'r he breaks.

When the dark night of death is done,
Come, Jesus Christ, shall be our call.
We'll need no light, no lamp, no sun,
For Christ himself shall be our all.

(Tune: HAMBURG)

†††

### For Such as These

For such as these the kingdom comes,
The weary and the wounded ones;
How bless'd are those who mourn and weep.
How bless'd the hungry and the meek.

For such as these the kingdom comes,
The helpless and forgotten ones;
How bless'd are those who mercy show.
How bless'd are those who sorrow know.

For such as these the kingdom comes,
And in God's love they find a home.
The broken and the last and least
Are honored guests at Christ's great feast.

For we, Your people, now we pray,
Saved by your love and called by Your grace;
Lord, give to us the eyes to see
Your kingdom here—and yet to be.
                              (Tune: GERMANY)


††† 


## May These Walls
*(For Parkwood Baptist Church, High Point, NC)*

Bricks and mortar, hands and labor
Day by day a building raise;
But the church of Christ our Savior
Grows with worship, work and praise.
For the saints who've gone before us,
Faithful servants, dreamers strong,
We who see their vision living
Join glad hearts in grateful song.

For the dreamers still among us
Who can see what's yet to be;
For the workers and the planners
Who make real the dreams we see;
For Your people, still committed
To Your gospel in this place;
For these gifts that have been given
Unto You be thanks and praise.

May these walls become a shelter
Rest along the journey's way;

Holy space where grace is practiced,
Welcome space where love holds sway.
May these walls never divide us,
May Your Spirit make us one.
May our hearts and doors be open—
Room enough for everyone.
(Tune: BEACH SPRING)

††† 

### Come, See the Fullness

God the Creator
Gave in abundance
All of the wonder
We now behold;
Colors of glory,
Everyday beauty,
Echo the story
Of God's deep love.

Bold as the sunlight,
Tender as nightfall,
Love shaped the heav'n's height;
Love filled the seas.
Love formed the flowers,
Called forth the living;
Marked out the hours
Of time to be.

Come, see the fullness—
Life we've been given;
Beauty and promise,
Mystr'y and hope.
Laughter and weeping,
Vision and purpose;
Friends for the keeping,
Strength for the road.

Open our hearts wide,
Teach us Your wisdom
Lest our days pass by
Empty and small.
May we be witness
With Your creation—
To Your great kindness
Given to all.
                    (Tune: BUNESSAN)

††† 

## Christ, Our Liberty
*(Commissioned for the 1993 General Assembly
of the Cooperative Baptist Fellowship)*

Once a people came together
Bound by faith and vision new;
With the wonder of the gospel
Came God's gift of freedom true;
Freed to follow Christ in service,
Freed to worship and to seek;
Conscience guided by God's Spirit,
God their sole authority.

Having suffered persecution
They now fought for freedom's cause
That our faith be freely chosen,
Not defined by human laws.
We their children are entrusted
With the dream they dared to dream,
Each one free to seek God's leading,
In our Lord our unity.

From our sin our Lord has freed us;
In our darkness light has shined.

In our pain his love brings healing,
Words of hope for humankind.
Still, so many live in shadows,
Hunger, hate, grief and despair;
Some forgotten, some unnoticed,
Some untouched by hands of care.

In our freedom God commands us
That we share God's gift of grace;
For the sake of God's creation
We seek vision for this day.
Like our fathers and our mothers
May we always faithful be;
In our dying, find our living,
Bound to Christ, our liberty.

(Tune: NETTLETON)

†††